ELECTRONIC MUSIC PRODUCTION

2ND EDITION

BY ALAN DOUGLAS

TAB BOOKS Inc.

BLUE RIDGE SUMMIT, PA. 17214

Other TAB books by the author:

No. 832   *The Electronic Musical Instrument Manual*

SECOND EDITION

FIRST PRINTING

Library of Congress Cataloging in Publication Data

Douglas, Alan Lockhart Monteith, 1899-
    Electronic music production.

    Includes index.
    1. Musical instruments, Electronic. 2. Electronic
music—History and criticism. I. Title.
ML1092.D59   1982   789.9   82-5911
ISBN 0-8306-1418-4 (pbk.)   AACR2

Front cover photo courtesy of Maplin Electronic Supplies, Rayleigh, Essex, England.

Contents

Preface

"Music was forced to shape for itself the material on which it works. Painting and sculpture find the fundamental character of their materials, form and colour, in nature itself, which they strive to imitate. Poetry finds its material ready formed in the words of language. Music alone finds an infinitely rich but totally shapeless plastic material in the tones of musical instruments. There is a greater and more absolute freedom in the use of material for music than for any of the other arts; but certainly it is more difficult to make a proper use of absolute freedom."

So wrote von Helmholtz in 1880. What remarkable insight and how very true.

The many forms through which music has passed through the ages indicate that there is a time and place for everything. When Wagner's "Tannhaüser" was first performed, an eminent critic wrote: "It seems to me that a man who will not only write such a thing, but actually have it printed, has little call for an artistic career." Today the public is more tolerant, and instead of being bound by convention is indeed very forward looking. Thus we can welcome the introduction of electronic music as a real entity, an art in its own right; and if Helmholtz's words are carefully studied, and we do not try to run before we can walk, this music will become as firmly established as is Tannhaüser. This is of course the danger; the whole art is so new, and everything associated with it is so fluid, that there is temptation to use the method just for the sake of the tremendous potential of a new creative medium. It will take time and experience for musicians to adjust their thinking in terms of the abstract, in terms of the basic ingredients of the sound instead of the finished sound itself.

It would not be possible to write a book of this kind without drawing on the experience of the pioneers of this art, and on the ingenuity of the circuit designers, who for the first time have become as important as the composers themselves. Grateful acknowledgment is therefore made to the following individuals and companies for the use of material first described by them, and for the use of certain diagrams or circuits.

Philips Technical Review, Vol. 19, No. 6, 1957.

Technische Hausmitteilungen NWDR, 8-15, 1954.

Journal of the Audio Engineering Society, New York, N.Y.

Music, Physics and Engineering, Dover Publications Inc, New York, N.Y., U.S.A.

The Wireless World, London, SE1.

IPC Magazines Ltd, London, SE1.

Electronics & Music Maker, Westcliffe on Sea, England.

Dr. Hugh le Caine, National Research Council, Ottawa, Canada.

Dr. Harry Olson, RCA Laboratories, Princeton, N.J., U.S.A.

Professor Milton Babbitt, Columbia University, New York, N.Y., U.S.A.

Max Matthews, Bell Laboratories, Murray Hill, N.J., U.S.A.

Daphne Oram, Tower Folly, Fairseat, Wrotham, Kent.

Robert A. Moog, Moog Laboratories, Trumansburg, N.Y., U.S.A.

Gustav Ciamaga, University of Toronto, Toronto, Canada.

Further references will be found in the Bibliography.

This is not a construction book in the sense that complete designs for pianos, organs, or synthesizers are shown. There is plenty of sophisticated technical literature on these subjects, but there is a scarcity of published material for the amateur, explaining in simple non-mathematical terms, how these circuits work, and how, by inexpensive means, the experimenter can build circuits which often give results equal to costly commercial instruments. It is hoped that this book will help the newcomer gain an understanding of the many facets of this new medium.

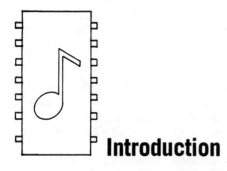

Introduction

Music has been produced in all countries and all civilizations since time immemorial. Elementary and vocal in origin, as instruments began to be developed so the complexity of the music increased. The Western world developed more rapidly than the East, and we find the means for composing and interpreting written music advancing at roughly the same rates. As composers required new tone colors and effects, these were provided by improved instruments.

This process continued into the 19th century, when physics could no longer provide extensions to the power, pitch or manipulative characteristics of conventional musical instruments. There were limits to these characteristics and composers had no alternative but to write within these limits. Convention was very strong and communication of musical ideas was only possible by concerts or by performances in the home. The ability to bring new music to the people was limited by these conditions.

With the advent of broadcasting the listening public increased enormously in number and, with the introduction of electrical gramophone recording, music in all forms could be studied and appreciated at any time or in any place. Nonetheless, conservatism in musical form or the geometry of composition was limited to well-known classical types of structure. The public was not ready for departures from existing practice.

Many early experimenters in all forms of art and science were frustrated by the lack of means to interpret their ideas. Many of us can recall the days when even to receive a broadcast called for some manipulative skill with sometimes uncertain results. Advances in electronics since the last war now provide powerful and stable tools with which to overcome many of the limitations of conventional instruments and to provide new ones. Art reflects the age in which it was born; today the means are there as well.

So now we must ask ourselves, why do we want these new devices, and what are we going to do with them?

We define electronic music as the production of waveforms by electrical oscillations, that is, the source is itself inaudible and is not in the form of air pressure waves, to which alone the ear can respond.

The oscillations, however generated, are then processed by electronic circuitry into desired forms which can be converted into audible sounds through the medium of electro-acoustic transducers, commonly one or more loudspeakers. So we can see that the distinguishing features of all electrically generated sounds are that the source itself cannot be heard, and that the initial oscillations or vibrations are of small amplitude, and therefore have little energy.

Since waveforms of a regularly recurring and cyclic pattern constitute music, while those of irregular, transient or spasmodic form constitute noise, it is easy to see that effects ranging from a pure tone (like a tuning fork) to bursts of noise (like a machine gun) can be generated by suitable electrical means, because today we are able to produce simultaneously any kind of oscillation of any frequency and as many as we need. Then, because of the universal use of the tape recorder, any form of subsequent processing, re-recording and storage is possible.

Music, of any nature whatsoever, derives from a combination of three parameters only: pitch, intensity, and duration. These can be broken down in a more precise and analytical way. To form a complete musical sound as at present understood requires a pitch or frequency, a rate at which the sound starts, a period over which it is maintained, and a rate at which it decays and disappears. Then there will be added harmonics, overtones or partials, probably noise due to the method of generation, and of course a loudness or intensity level (not necessarily fixed). Additionally, there may be second-order effects such as reverberation and vibrato.

It is evident that a parameter such as frequency can be exactly specified, but any factor depending on a time scale is less precise. For this reason, conventional notation can only delineate pitch or frequency with any real accuracy, the absolute value of a written note being related to the absolute value of other notes in a rather loose way. The envelope characteristics are even more difficult to specify. This expression embraces the whole period of time for which the note is sounding, and includes the starting time, the holding time and the decay time. Since these attributes are also bound up with the intensity or loudness, it can be seen that envelope control is both complex and important. In all these basic respects, electronic music generators can prove much superior and infinitely more flexible than any conventional music generator.

We will see in Chapter 1 that the introduction of harmonics to color the pitch note is almost entirely dependent on the physical properties of the instrument, and of course this is the exact opposite of electronically produced sound where there is no timbre until specified and inserted by the operator, with the exception of elementary apparatus for experimental purposes.

Electronic music falls into several classes: tone production, composing, and direct or live performance. None of these fields suffer from the limitations imposed on or by conventional musical instruments. Yet, because of the long established status of the orchestral instrument, we should see how the sounds derived from such instruments are produced, and what shortcomings they may have. For it is one of the aims of electronic music to overcome these deficiencies, some of which are explained later.

It might be thought that a prime aim of electronic music was to displace the human performer entirely in the course of time. Of course, there are schools of thought with this in mind; nevertheless, it seems highly improbable that this will ever come about, and it is much more likely that electronic music and composition per se will provide another art form having its own language, performers, and devotees.

Let us then look at some of the limitations of conventional physical instruments. Ever since the introduction of temperament, or any form of relating the various notes of the scale, many instruments have been designed with valves or keys producing fixed intervals between adjacent notes. It is clear that such a construction is an essential part of a piano or organ, and it is employed in all woodwind and brass instruments except the trombone. Music must conform with these intervals to be playable at all. But this construction confers one very great advantage—it is unfailingly repetitive, that is, pressing the same key will always produce the same note. This enables music to be written with accuracy.

At the same time, we have the string family, which is characterized by having no fixed intervals; one can play a quarter tone, tenth tone, or any other fraction. This family, then, though capable of playing any pitch within its limits, must still conform to the fixed temperament of other instruments. It is evident at once that if other instruments could be made to play in any desired fraction of an interval (of the existing temperament) a vast number of new musical forms and patterns would become available. And, of course, we find just these properties in the synthesizer.

Next, there is the question of power or loudness output from any individual instrument. Detailed information on this is given later, but obviously there is a limit to the degree of vibration possible, whether it be a string or an air column. For more power one must therefore have more instruments. This at once leads to possible lack of accuracy in interpreting, and certainly differences in harmonic texture or timbre between individuals in a group.

Then consider the pitch range. This must be limited by the need for compactness and ease of manipulation, apart from the fact that the stimulating energy must be imparted by human means and the performer has limited stamina. Moreover, in nearly every conventional instrument, there are marked differences in both the power and quality of the extreme upper and lower notes, so that one cannot really exploit the full range of notes possible with equal effect. In any case, no one instrument can cover the whole compass of notes required for that quality of sound—the violin must give way to the viola, then the 'cello, then the bass viol to cover the possible range required by the composer for string tone. It would be very desirable to overcome these limitations and extend the composer's powers.

Let us then approach the question of noise and non-musical sounds accompanying the tone band. Virtually all orchestral instruments depend on resonant systems to develop the power required. It is well known that much more power is required to start a coupled system resonating than to maintain it in that condition, but it is not possible to reduce the energy by much once it has been applied. The excess power then appears as noise. This is very marked in bowed instruments, particularly where the tone band is widely separated from the noise band, as in the bass viol for example, or where the applied power must always be great to get the instrument to speak at all, as in the piccolo.

There are clicks from valves and noise from the impact of piano or xylophone hammers, and excessive wind noise from the organ. When a mute is used on a violin, the bowing noise may be almost as great as the tone engendered. We accept these imperfections because we have been brought up with them, but this is not to say it is a good thing.

No instrument depending on resonance can release its energy instantly, though it may start vibrating almost at once if enough force is applied; so there is a natural rate of attack and decay for all conventional instruments. If damping is applied to bring about a quicker cessation of the sound, then the shape of the decay curve is altered and the effect is often unreal. Many new musical effects are possible if there is control over the starting and stopping rates of a musical sound and this is possible by electronic means.

Lastly, the range of musical percussions is limited with physical instruments; there is a big gap here in the orchestral spectrum, easily filled electronically. The same applies to non-musical percussions, e.g., triangle, drums, wood blocks, cymbals, etc. The difficulty of getting a cymbal to ring continuously, for instance, is readily solved by synthetic means.

If we add the whole of these possible limitations together, coupled with the difficulty of manipulating many instruments (and even the uncertainty, as in the French horn), we shall see in this book that in addition to overcoming them by electronic means, we are able to vastly increase the power and pitch range; obtain crescendos and diminuendos impossible with conventional instruments; divide the scaling into an infinite number of parts; obtain any degree of glissando or sliding scale; form completely new tone colors; supply echo or reverberation to any required extent and vary this at any instant as may be needed; produce arpeggios or similar progressions at a greater rate than is possible by human agency; and certainly in some cases, make the technique of playing a particular instrument very much easier. In short, to open up a whole new world of possibilities to the composer who cares to take advantage of these methods.

Although the original purpose of this book was directed towards more serious or classical music, the advent of microelectronics in the form of integrated circuits has made the construction of synthesizing instruments for direct or live playing, possible; because of compactness and light weight. So, apart from organesque instruments, which have been with us for many years, we find a new generation of keyboard instruments from which not only synthesized orchestral tones but many quite new ones are at the performer's fingertips; sometimes with startling effect, as sophisticated percussion circuits develop. In addition, deliberate distortion of musical sounds and effects is popular in certain circles, so we have devoted some space to all these ideas. Some of these attributes cannot be described in existing musical terminology, a special kind of language has developed for these effects.

Some space is devoted in this book to composing by mechanical means, but it is not thought possible ever to dispense with the human brain. Science can greatly aid the musician today, but science and art do not speak the same language and it would be disastrous if music became completely automated.

In my opinion, it is a combination of the conventional and the unconventional which will extract the best from music in times to come; and this would appear to agree with future economic as well as artistic trends.

Chapter 1

Properties of Conventional Musical Instruments

Now we have said that one purpose of electronic music is to extend, by means of synthesis, the range and quality of established orchestral instruments. So it as well to understand how the quality of tone associated with a particular instrument is produced. The construction, mechanism and materials used, as well as the method of playing or manipulation, all influence the final sound spectrum.

Synthesis of some instruments is difficult and confers no advantage over the physical instrument. But some have gross defects, extreme difficulty in playing, and an uneven frequency response. Firstly it is as well to remember that no known orchestral instrument maintains its fundamental pitch and the *same* retinue of harmonics for more than a second or so. Every change in loudness or in pitch is accompanied by a change in the harmonic structure. This is because of the delicacy in control exercised by the player, the net effect being to prevent monotony of tone and to heighten the aesthetic appeal. This statement must be related to the form and purpose of the music being played, as witness the differing interpretations of the same piece of music under different conductors, using the same instruments. Let us look briefly at how some of the principal families of tone are produced.

THE OBOE

This instrument consists of a small mouthpiece holding an exposed reed, which is immersed in the breath of the player. The reed is attached to the narrow end of a slightly conical tube. The reed is double or consists of one reed doubled back on itself, and is made from thin cane, as shown in Fig. 1-1. It can vibrate both transversely and longitudinally. In the course of such vibrations, the small gap at the top end is alternately opened and closed,

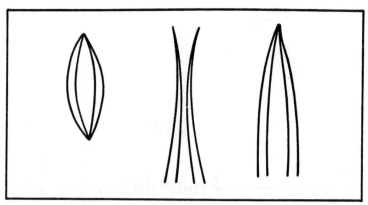

Fig. 1-1. Oboe reed.

allowing pulses of air from the player's mouth to pass into the upper or narrow end of the tube which forms the body of the instrument. This latter controls the pitch note, the tones proper to the reed itself being much higher in pitch. Wood is used for the construction, and this is of great rigidity. When an air column is in a state of vibration in any constraining device such as a pipe or tube, should there be any tendency for the walls of the tube to be elastic, the intensity of any harmonic happening to have an antinode near to the point of flexure will be reduced in amplitude, since part of the energy of the wave will be used to deform the wall of the tube; the tone will sound duller and will lose carrying power.

The conical form of the tube permits the full harmonic series of tones being developed, in spite of the fact that the tube is substantially closed at the upper end. This harmonic series is of course necessary properly to reinforce the characteristic tone of the reed, but the excitation of these various modes is governed by the so-called "formant" frequencies of the whole system. It is well known that each kind of vibration device has a band of frequencies which predominates no matter what fundamental or pitch note is being played. These fixed bands appear for every note within the compass of the instrument, and in Fig. 1-2 we can see some of the more common formant bands for different instruments. These should be noted, since synthesis of many orchestral sounds involves the creation of formant bands by means of electrical resonant circuits. The materials of which the resonating tube is made are mainly responsible for the composition of a particular formant group, and certainly it is this which gives the shrill yet plaintive tone to the oboe, for, since all harmonics can be excited in the body, unless this were so the tone would be much smoother and rounder, there being no particular reason why one harmonic should be more prominent than another.

It might not seem very relevant to note the process by which a cone open at the base only can produce practically the full series of harmonics, that is, the equivalent of a parallel pipe open at both ends, but this gives an important clue as to why a change in geometry can alter the propositions, number and power of harmonics in instrument resonators. By combining a conical tube with a cylindrical parallel tube so that the major control is due to either one or the other form of tube; or by proportioning the fractions of each tube in an empirical way brought about by experiment, the harmonics proper to the vibrator or to the air column may be reinforced; or, it may be possible to force the air column to produce some series of partials which may not be strictly harmonic. It is this desirability of balancing one state against another state, over as wide a range of pitch and power as possible, which accounts for the fact that almost every orchestral wind instrument has a resonating tube combining, in part, the properties of a cone and a parallel cylinder.

Without deriving the full equations for the above conditions as applied to the oboe and taking R as the slant length of the cone, N_m as the frequency of the mth natural harmonic, λ_m as its wavelength and a as the speed of sound, we have:

$$R = m\lambda_m/2 \text{ or } N_m = ma/2R$$

giving almost the same fundamental and full harmonic series of tones as from a parallel pipe of the same length open at both ends. We might note in

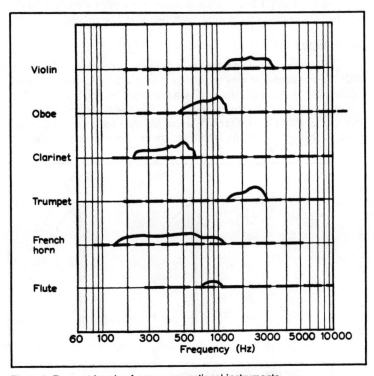

Fig. 1-2. Formant bands of some conventional instruments.

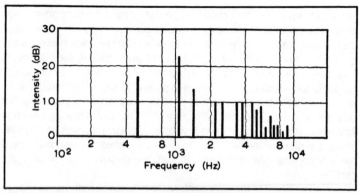

Fig. 1-3. Spectrum of orchestral oboe at frequency of 523 Hz.

passing that the oboe is little affected by temperature, the percentage increase in frequency of the instrument for a rise of 10° F is only 0.31, about one half of that of other instruments. For this reason it is used as a pitch standard for tuning other orchestral instruments. Moreover, its penetrating quality of tone is readily heard above the sound of other instruments.

Finally, in Fig. 1-3 we show a characteristic harmonic analysis for $f = 523$ Hz. The comparatively weak fundamental will be noticed.

THE CLARINET

Although at first sight the oboe and clarinet appear very alike physically, the mechanism of tone production is quite different. The tube of the clarinet is cylindrical and the reed is of the single beating type, as in Fig. 1-4, which shows the reed open and closed. It is also made from cane but is much wider than the oboe reed. Whereas the oboe reed opens and closes more or less symmetrically with time, the reed of the clarinet tends to

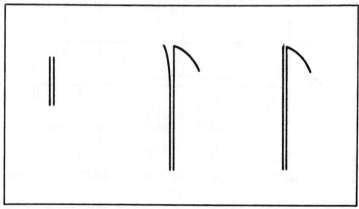

Fig. 1-4. Clarinet reed, open and closed.

4

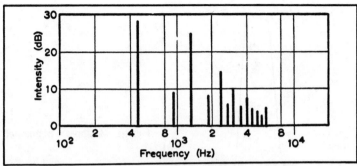

Fig. 1-5. Spectrum of orchestral clarinet at frequency of 465 Hz.

remain closed for a long time in any one cycle of operations, then opens rapidly to the full extent. The body is made from very hard wood and can also be made of metal; the tone is then harder and louder than that of a wooden one, as is to be expected from the reduced internal damping and the higher rate of transmission of sound waves in metal. Since the tube has parallel walls, plane waves are propagated, and hence the reed end of the tube is a node; only odd harmonics will be radiated, although there are small traces of even ones as well. The fundamental tone is about three times as powerful as the most significant formant tone. This is because the reed is broad, and the hollow-sounding nature of an odd harmonic system tends to be apparently more full and mellow than one in which all harmonics are engendered. Note, however, that while the oboe maintains its peculiar quality over the whole compass, the tone of the clarinet becomes harder in the upper register. A frequency spectrum of a typical clarinet is shown in Fig. 1-5.

THE TRUMPET

This is an instrument of the "labial" type, in which there is no actual reed, the lips of the player taking its place. It has the reputation of being the most brilliant of the brass instruments, but this is to some extent due to the pitch range, which is in a favorable position for stimulating the ear. The actual power output in fact is much less than that of the trombone. A high blowing pressure is required to force the air in the 6 ft long tube into resonance with the lips. Figure 1-6 shows the cupped mouthpiece having rings spun into the tube to form constrictions. The action of these is as follows.

When a jet of air issues from a circular orifice there is a tendency for it to curl up into vortex rings. These can be ranged into an orderly procession by making the issuing air strike an edge. In this case it is a circular edge. The distances between successive vortices then becomes equal to, or a sub-multiple of, the distance from the orifice of the jet to the circular edge facing it. The pitch of the note due to the vortices striking the edge is related to the velocity of the jet and with the distance from orifice to edge.

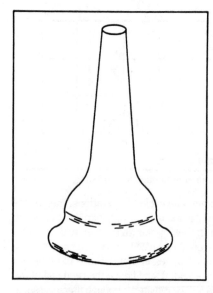

Fig. 1-6. Mouthpiece of trumpet.

By making this last distance very small, we can get very high pitched notes. The formula for the normal production of these edge tones then becomes

$$\text{Pitch of edge tone} = \frac{\frac{1}{3} \text{ (Velocity of issuing breath)}}{\text{Distance from lips to mouthpiece flange}}$$

So to produce a high note the player should press the lips in towards the flange as well as increase the speed or pressure of his breath; and of course the tension on the lips must be increased as well.

The material of which the tube is made influences the tone; brass is common, silver produces a duller tone. In all cases the last foot or so rapidly expands into a flared mouth. A harmonic spectrum of a trumpet is given in Fig. 1-7. The sound is easily synthesized electrically with many variants.

THE FLUTE

Sounds of this nature are the most commonly synthesized, for the obvious reason that they are very simple and very easily generated. But one must beware of this apparent simplicity, for indeed orchestral flute tone contains many harmonics with many shades of expression. The tone-producing elements consist of a circular orifice forming an edge tone generator, closely coupled to an adjustable resonating tube. The player blows, not into but across the circular mouth hole, so that his breath strikes the opposite edge. The more massive air column in the tube reinforces the harmonics proper to the particular pitch, and extinguishes any other overtones purely due to the edge tone though these can be clearly heard if one approaches the player closely. But the tone quality is quite different in the different octaves. This is because to extend the range, the blowing pressure

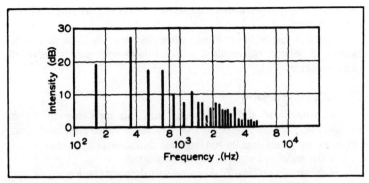

Fig. 1-7. Spectrum of orchestral trumpet at frequency of 175 Hz.

increased, so that the edge tone jumps up an octave, when the same note holes in the tube are used again; and yet again to complete the top octave. It is in this harmonic generation process that the quality of the sound becomes different, for the following reasons.

The small reduction in tube diameter near the mouth hole causes the pitch of the overtones to be slightly lowered, and the higher the pitch, the greater this effect. So that, since the second and third octaves are obtained from overtones of the fundamental by over-blowing, there will be a disproportionate rise in pitch as the frequency rises. There is a device in the air column to allow of fractional tuning of the resonator, but this does not bring the system completely into tune. The player may however do so by lip and breath manipulation at his discretion. And as the pitch of these notes is forced nearer to or further from the harmonic series of the tube, the quality of the sound changes in a way determined by the playing technique. Therefore, in Fig. 1-8 we show loud, medium and soft tones to show how the

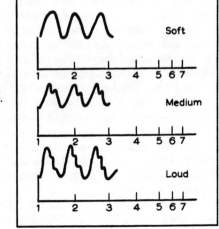

Fig. 1-8. Analysis of flute tone.

7

harmonic content varies with pitch and power. It is clear that true synthesis is very difficult.

Research carried out in France using electronic methods, notably by Buffet and Selmer, has resulted in metal flutes with greatly improved characteristics.

STRINGED INSTRUMENTS

With the exception of the trombone, wind instruments have fixed pitch intervals determined by the position of the holes or valves in the air column. However, by exceptional lip and fingering ability, skilled players can produce a glissando on certain of these instruments.

In the string family we find several very different features. In the first place, they are all capable of an infinite pitch series depending only on the ability of the performer; save that the lowest pitch is always fixed by the lowest natural frequency of the string in use and the dimensions of the body or resonator. Secondly, quite different kinds of tone quality can be obtained from each instrument, by bowing in different ways or by plucking the strings; by striking them and by using a mute. So there is enormous versatility in use, virtually unlimited, and for this reason it is difficult to specify a set of conditions which truly represent any vibratile state of the violin, violincello or bass viol.

It must be made clear that the purpose of the strings is to drive the body of the instrument, since by themselves they radiate no energy to the air; their small cross-section allows the air to flow round them unhindered, and no sound comes from them, certainly not for more than a few inches away. However, the strings are made from certain specified materials to regularize bowing technique and to impart enough energy to the body. This latter moves a large amount of free air and so transmits sufficient energy to be heard at a distance. The aim of the designer is to make the body act as a sounding board and not a resonator.

Without going into the theory of the system, it should be noted that the width of the bow may be comparable with the length of the string for many frequencies, which will not then sound; if the string is plucked with a sharp object, such as the finger nail, these frequencies will sound and the tone becomes harder and sharper. Many of these effects can be synthesized as we shall see later on. A typical spectrum of a violin sounding a quite steady note is given in Fig. 1-9. The functioning of the violincello and bass viol is quite similar, except that in the latter, the dimensions of the body do not often encourage the proper development of the very lowest notes, which sound weak.

It is noteworthy that a trained violinist will play in perfect pitch, so that during a violin solo with piano accompaniment it has been thought that the discrepancy in pitch is a fault in intonation; but in fact it is the piano which is wrong, as we shall see.

It is not necessary to go into the theory underlying the action of a stretched string, for those interested there are ample references at the end

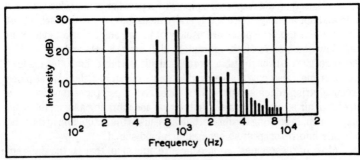

Fig. 1-9. Spectrum of violin at frequency of 294 Hz.

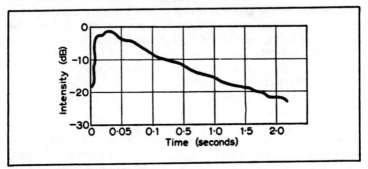

Fig. 1-10. Decay curve of guitar.

of this book. Suffice it to say that research on the properties of the viole family has occupied many investigators for a long time, but nothing of a practical nature which was not known to the violin makers of two hundred years ago appears to have come from this work.

The guitar may be bracketed with violes, since it employs stretched strings. However, the strings are heavier and the body is larger for the pitch range. The strings also terminate on a flexible bridge, and the whole acoustic system is more yielding, so that a louder sound is produced and there is an appreciable delay in the cessation of the sound, as in Fig. 1-10. Of course, a bow is not used and it is usual to provide frets or bars positioned to indicate the position for stopping the strings for various notes. Today the electric guitar permits a quite different tonal spectrum because the vibrations are picked up by magnetic means and the body has no influence on the tone quality. Since the pickups are very sensitive, the vibrations may continue much longer than with the acoustic instrument, where the energy soon falls below the level required to excite the soundboard.

THE PIPE ORGAN

This is not a book on the organ, so we will only deal with some of the characteristics open to synthesis in a general way. The church or concert organ is based on the diapason, a pipe with a peculiar sound which is not a flute and not a string; there are literally thousands of different schools of diapason voicing. The pipes are usually of metal, and cover a range from very low notes of 16 Hz to extremely high ones, 8 kHz and above. The theater organ rests on the tibia chorus, and this is a large flute often made of wood. It may also cover a very wide range of pitch. Other metal pipes produce string tones and pure flute tones. All these pipes function by a stream of air issuing from a slot in the pipe and vibrating a lip on the main tube, which, in starting to vibrate, quickly causes the air column in the tube to come into resonance, so generating a loud sound.

Most of these pipes are in octave relationship, that is, the different tonal effects are of 16, 8, 4 and 2 ft pitches; but a very important group of pipes is to be found in the mixtures and mutations. Because the larger and more powerful of the diapasons tend to be poor in harmonic development, additional ranks inject these missing harmonics and in fact allow control of the total number of harmonics present by adjusting the number of these extra ranks. We therefore find that pitches of 10.2/3, 5.1/3, 2.2/3, 1.3/5 and still more complex fractions may be present and these can be used to greatly heighten the value of the flue pipes constituting the main body of sound. The use of such fractional pitches will be examined when we look at electrical synthesis.

In addition to the pipes just mentioned, there are many imitating reed sounds, some conventional such as the oboe, trumpet or clarinet, some exclusive to the organ, such as the tuba, tromba and ophicleide. All of these function by having a vibrating metal reed in an enclosure which holds the reed firmly and at the same time prevents the sound of the actual reed from being heard. A resonating tube attached to the top of the reed assembly, or boot as it is called, emphasizes the proper pitch note of the pipe and reduces or eliminates the discordant harmonics which would otherwise be heard—as for example in the harmonium, where the reeds are not supplied with resonators and have a rather harsh sound as a consequence. By way of illustration, we show the spectrum of a vibrating reed alone, Fig. 1-11, and the same reed when attached to a tuned pipe, Fig. 1-12. The "filtering" action of the pipe is evident.

One aspect of the open metal pipe should be mentioned, as it is most difficult to synthesize. All pipes must be mounted, and of course there has to be a value to admit wind when required. The geometry of this system greatly influences the rate and the manner in which the pipe speaks. If we consider a pipe standing on a wind chest, there will be static air in the foot of the pipe when at rest. This foot is only a support and takes no part in tone production, but it can hold a lot of air in a large pipe, and this must be driven out before the wind reaches the lip. Clearly any pipe has mass, which has to be set into vibration by a suddenly applied puff of wind. This cannot be instantaneous, and when the valve is first opened, the rush of wind causes a momentary false transient to appear, often audibly. As the wind continues to flow, the transient gradually becomes weaker as the lip begins to vibrate. During the rise in amplitude of the vibrations of the pipe the apparent

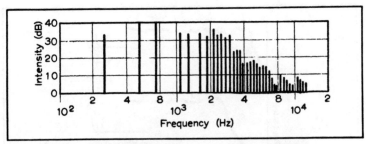

Fig. 1-11. Spectrum of reed tongue alone at frequency of 262 Hz.

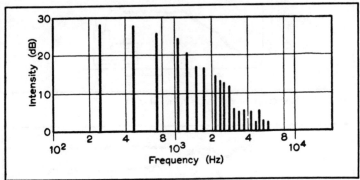

Fig. 1-12. Spectrum of reed tongue plus resonating tube at frequency of 262 Hz.

frequency of the vibration is neither that of the transient or that of the exciting force; it is a variable composite of the two which approaches the steady-state frequency as the transient disappears. Figure 1-13 shows how the geometry of a pipe and valve assembly can affect the starting of the sound, and in Fig. 1-14 we can see what actually happens on admission of the wind to a pipe—that is, after it has been through the valve passage.

We have instanced this starting transient as a function of the flue organ pipe, but it exists in any system set into forced vibration and is noticeable in struck or plucked strings. It can be eliminated by electrical means.

THE PIANOFORTE

Today we have a great number of electrical percussion circuits by means of which piano and similar effects can be synthesized, sometimes so well that they cannot be detected. Nevertheless, the total effect is not that of the piano, and perhaps we should see what makes the conventional piano sound as it does.

Generally, from tenor C upwards, there is little to distinguish one piano from another. It is in the bass that there is a great difference, and this is because of the size of the soundboard. Since we know that the strings themselves cannot radiate any energy, it is obvious that the larger the bass

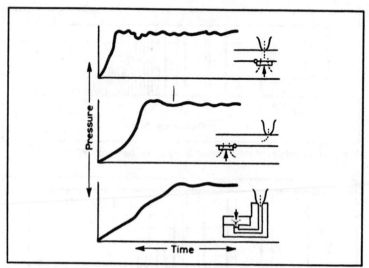

Fig. 1-13. Influence of air valves on inflow of wind.

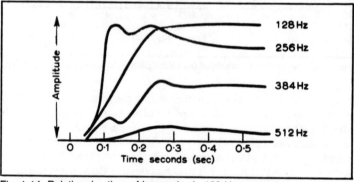

Fig. 1-14. Relative rise time of harmonics in 128 Hz organ pipe.

area of the soundboard, the better the effect on the ear. This explains the shape of the grand piano, and as we will see when we look at the sensitivity curves of the ear, much more energy is needed at the lower end of the compass to give equal loudness.

The frequencies of the partials of a struck string are not truly harmonics of the fundamental frequency, and such partials are progressively sharpened as their order increases. This "inharmonicity" is not the same for all strings, being least in the middle of the keyboard and increasing towards the bottom and the top. It is most pronounced at the upper end, and this is not surprising since the top strings, being so short and stiff, are really more like bars than strings. Because of the differences in mass and tension, we find a mistuning effect as in Fig. 1-15 for an average grand piano, since

12

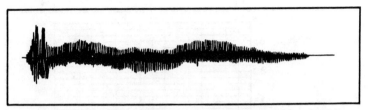

Fig. 1-15. Mistuning between piano strings on striking a note C = 523 Hz.

tuners depend on the rate of beating of certain intervals for the accuracy of tempering the scale. This effect is very real as can be seen from Fig. 1-16 which shows the average of sixteen pianos examined. Note here that one cent is one hundredth of a semitone, so there are 1200 cents to an octave; one cent is equal to a frequency difference of 0.06%. For the reasons given, the effect of sustaining many consecutive chords in the extreme upper or lower registers would become displeasing in a very short time. With a long string, even when damped by the mechanism provided, the sound does not cease immediately, and when the dampers are removed by the sustaining pedal, the string may vibrate for a long time, as in Fig. 1-17. This is the Mid C string, but of course there are no single strings in the instrument, except in the bass, and the effect of the three strings settling down after striking is very complex, adding a further difficulty to any method of synthesis. Firstly they vibrate in phase, but soon they begin to vibrate in a random manner because the mass and tension cannot be exactly the same for every string. It is this kind of fractional deviation which gives the richness of tone to a good piano.

Now there is one very important characteristic of the piano, the percussive starting tone. Examination of a piano waveform always shows a very steep rise, of a transient nature, to the start of the wave. But the oscillations of the string do not contain any transients. The effect is due to a rotational movement of the bridge axis at the moment of striking the string, as a result of the sudden relief of strain in this member. That such a transient does exist is easily proved by electrical pickups. At no point on the string can this sharp impact sound be obtained, but if a pickup is placed on the bridge the sound becomes percussive, see Fig. 1-18.

"Electric" pianos have been made, in which the sound is removed from the strings by a series of pickups, but they do not sound very like pianos; it is necessary to have some soundboard to stop the strings from continuing to vibrate indefinitely, yet not enough to act as a loudspeaker to excite the pickups in a spurious manner. It is very difficult to play such a piano, examples of which were produced by Nernst, Bechstein, Vierling and Forster.

These rather cumbersome adaptations gradually turned into devices where, for example, the hammer struck a metal reed; or held on to it by suction until the restoring force of the reed let it go; in either case there was a magnetic pickup at one end of the reed (incidentally this gives a note of

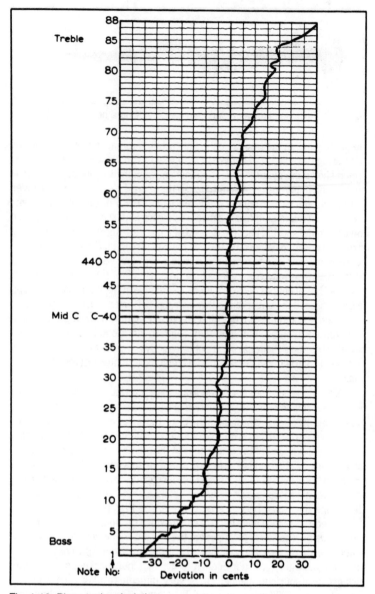

Fig. 1-16. Piano tuning deviation.

twice the actual frequency of the reed); but all such pianos have succumbed to the purely electronic types, examples of which are given later on.

In considering the harp, the only real difference is the absence of a proper soundboard, requiring the strings to be stopped by hand. Otherwise

14

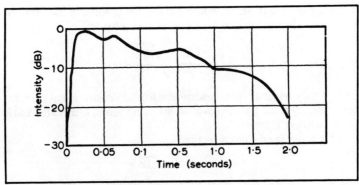

Fig. 1-17. Decay curve for piano.

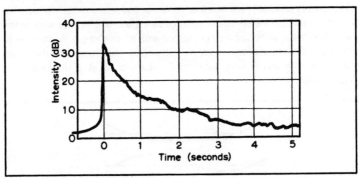

Fig. 1-18. Percussive start of piano tone.

the vibrations would persist for a long time, allowing notes to run into each other. The resultant tone quality depends very greatly on the point at which the string is plucked. If it were plucked in the center, all even partials would be absent from the tone; if plucked at one seventh from the end this and all other partials having a node at this point would be suppressed, and the tone would be smoother and more agreeable. Again, if the finger is used, the angle is less acute where the string is plucked than if a sharp point were used, therefore the latter would invoke a harder and more nasal tone.

The vibrations begin to die away as soon as the string is released, but the higher order ones decay much faster than the lower ones, so the sound appears more pleasant to the ear as it persists. Thus, the player has several ways of modifying the sound spectrum.

THE GLOCKENSPIEL

The glockenspiel, celesta, and dulcitone represent types of percussion instruments using metal bars struck by hammers. Such bars must be thin compared with their vibrating length to ensure they will only vibrate in one plane. Otherwise the tone quality is a very complex mixture of odd partials. Figure 1-19 shows a free bar and the position of the first few overtones. The fundamental frequency of such a bar is:

$$f_1 = \frac{1.33}{l^2} \sqrt{\frac{QK^2}{p}}$$

where l is the length of bar in centimeters; p is the density, grams per cubic centimeter; Q is the Young's modulus, dynes per square centimeter; and K is the radius of gyration.

For a rectangular cross-section,

$$K = \pm aP \sqrt{12}$$

where a is the thickness of the bar in centimeters.

The bar is of course supported at the two nodes nearest to the free ends, usually on small pads of felt or by cords, and struck at the center. The fundamental is very weak when mounted on a frame in free air, owing to the small size of the radiating area compared with a wavelength. As the rate of exchange of operating force is great, owing to the hard hammers, the sound starts instantly and is very incisive. The bars being stiff, the vibrations decay rapidly too.

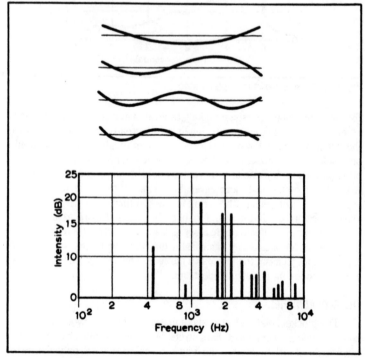

Fig. 1-19. Spectrum of glockenspiel.

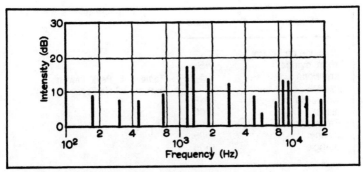

Fig. 1-20. Spectrum of cymbal at frequency of 175 Hz.

ATONAL INSTRUMENTS

These are used as rhythm markers and are not music makers but noise generators. Their chief characteristic is an immediate and percussive attack, with various forms of decay curve, but most may be sustained by reiteration, that is, constantly hitting the device to keep it vibrating.

The triangle is a steel bar of circular section bent into the form of a triangle, but not completely closed. The cross-section may vary throughout the length of the bar. From its construction, it is obvious that it can vibrate transversely, longitudinally or torsionally, and all these vibrations may super-impose themselves on one another. The net result is a closely packed vibration pattern of high partials (there can be no low ones on account of the short length of the bar,) and these are both harmonic and inharmonic. It is largely because there are so many high inharmonic tones that the triangle can be heard above a full orchestra, since there are gaps in the total sound spectrum into which these partials can obtrude. Somewhat similar sounds can be synthesized quite well; they are not the same but quite acceptable.

The cymbal is the other important rhythm marker, also a noise generator; but the partials are of a quite different kind. The circular brass plate is supported at the center, which must then be a node for all vibrations. The diameter is considerable, producing a large sound output in the high frequency range; by far the largest amount of energy is radiated from 5000 Hz upwards, indeed, far above audibility. The vibrations of the plate are very complex and are always inharmonic; it would be possible to vibrate the plate in one of its major modes if it were perfectly balanced and of uniform stress distribution. There is no real steady state for the sound, even with reiteration, but it can be analysed and a part of its spectrum is shown in Fig. 1-20. Synthesis yields a very tolerable imitation, but it is only acceptable in the absence of the original. The power output in the range shown is so great that a single cymbal will stand out loud and clear above the orchestra; but enclosure or shielding of the instrument will remove the upper overtones, as indeed is the case with most musical instruments.

It is of interest to note the peak power outputs of some of the more common orchestral instruments. This gives a clue as to possible electrical

17

Source	Power, watts
75 piece orchestra	75
15 in. cymbal	9•5
trombone	6•5
trumpet	0•6
violincello	0•16
flute	0•06
French horn	0•05
clarinet	0•05
triangle	0•05

Table 1-1. Peak Powers Over the Whole Spectrum.

powers required for simulation; if one takes the efficiency of a really good loudspeaker properly mounted at 10%, then amplifiers having continuous power ratings of ten times the figures shown would be satisfactory. Usually additional power is in reserve in case of difficult acoustic conditions. See Table 1-1.

Chapter 2

Musical Scales, Temperament and Tuning, Concord and Discord

Generally, sounds which are smooth, regular, pleasant, and harmonious, and which either together or singly appeal to the ear may be classed as musical. But certain sounds of the same nature sounded together may give rise to an unpleasant sensation. We call the former concordant, the latter discordant. The octave is the basis for measurement and although only containing 12 notes, has been subdivided into 1200 parts called cents to attain some degree of accuracy. There are accordingly 100 cents to the semitone, which is the smallest interval of the musical scale for Western countries and the smallest which can conveniently be written on paper.

HARMONICS

No conventional musical sound has any value unless it contains some harmonics as well as the fundamental or pitch note. These harmonics should arise naturally from the vibratile characteristics of the instrument, and the most accurate and pleasing ones derive from a stretched string. If this is bowed correctly, analysis shows that the tones engendered are in the ratios 1, 2, 3, 4, 5, 6 etc.; this is called a harmonic series. If the bowing is continuous, at all other frequency intervals there are discordant sounds, which vanish at the exact points where the frequency ratios are found to be 5:4, 4:3, 3:2 and 2:1. It is a general law that two tones sound well together when the ratios of their frequencies can be expressed in small numbers. If we look at Table 2-1, we can see the increasing dissonance, so that the further we go from small numbers, the worse the discord. The well-known dissonance curve of von Helmholtz shows this perhaps more clearly, Fig. 2-1 where one violin sounds c_1 continuously while the other one moves gradually from c_1 to c_2.

Table 2-1. Frequency Ratio Versus Dissonance.

Note	Frequency ratio	ET interval error, cents	
C	1	0	0
D	9:8	200	4b
E	5:4	400	14#
F	4:3	500	2#
G	3:2	700	2b
A	5:3	900	16#
B	15:8	1100	12#
C	2:1	1200	0

Evidently the only two tones which cannot introduce any possible disturbance are those of the octave, which is the ratio 2:1. The tones which are the next most agreeable have frequencies in the ratio 3:2, or, 1·5. Thus, sounding one pair of such notes would be agreeable, and so would one or two more pairs; but eventually, as we have 12 notes in the octave, if we increased each step (or note) by the factor 1·5, we would have a value of 129·5. This is not exactly the value of the note (c) constituting the octave, it should be 128. Now we are a quarter of a semitone too high, and if this were continued, we would find that still higher notes ran far away from true pitch and resulted in discord. So some other solution must be sought. Neglecting the various mean tone and other methods of scaling which were in use at one time, the solution was found to lie in equal temperament tuning (which was proposed as long ago as 1482). Now, to obtain a frequency ratio of 128:1, each step must represent one twelfth of that, $\sqrt[12]{128}$ or 1·4983. All semitones are now equal, and each represents exactly the same frequency ratio. Within an octave this is the twelfth root of two, or 1·05945.

Now clearly some intervals must still sound better than others, and in certain keys there may be a loss of purity as compared with the mean tone or just scale; that this is a very real effect is shown by the scaling adopted by violinists and many vocalists; continuous monitoring of the spectrum shows

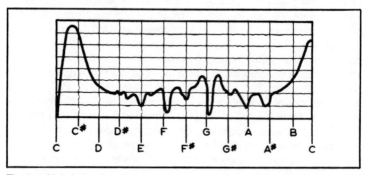

Fig. 2-1. Helmholtz dissonance curve.

these performers to depart from the equal scale to a considerable extent to secure purity of tone. Of course, in tuning certain instruments having keyboards, e.g., the piano and the organ, there may well be further stretching of the intervals to modify the effect of dissonant harmonics in the instrument.

Musical instruments can produce discords between themselves, even if properly tuned. If they have widely differing harmonic contents, then when two contrasting chords are played simultaneously, according to the relative position of the pitch notes, the harmonics would beat in quite different ways. These are determined by the harmonic ratios of the pitch notes, expressed as intervals; as indicated in Fig. 2-2. The harmonics are the black notes and the inversion of the two instruments clearly shows how quite different harmonic groups are engendered for the same chords. Orchestrators are very careful about arrangements for wood-wind sections and these are always limited in power compared to string and brass sections.

We have devoted some space to these matters because it must be clear that to synthesize musical sound by the addition of sine waves tuned to the intervals of the equally tempered scale would lead to very dubious results after the 6th harmonic. A third for example is a ratio of 1·2599, but a true third is 1·250; the tempered fifth is 1·4983, and is low in the ratio 1·4983:1·5 or approximately 881:882. Naturally, the sound from any instrument rich in harmonics would greatly complicate the above, which are related to pure waves only. It is clearly possible by electronic means to provide tone sources where the intervals could be flattened or sharpened at will, indeed it is only where conventional keyboards, wind valves or holes etc., are concerned, that the equal temperament scale need apply. When one looks at this convention, it is apparent that the real reason for the intervals as we

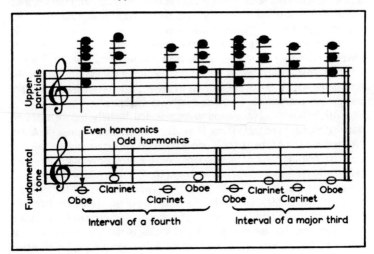

Fig. 2-2. Beats due to unequal harmonic texture.

know them is to allow a human being to span the controlling apparatus comfortably. Twelve keys to the octave are satisfactory; 25 keys would not be possible. But there is no limit to the gradations of the scale where electronic music is concerned. Any possible limitation is only because of the difficulty of committing the music to paper. As we shall see later, this is by no means necessary in all cases.

It has, in fact, been proposed to have a 53 note scale, which would give true fifths as well as all the other intervals, including the all-important third. But even this is slightly imperfect and this is only the more reason why electronic frequencies should be generated as continuous gliding tones, to be dissected and combined as required. There are ways of annotating this kind of spectrum, although perhaps not immediately intelligible; but then, is conventional music intelligible to anyone not trained to interpret it?

NOTATION

The various ways of notationally conveying the composers' intentions to the performer as employed in conventional music scores may prove to be totally inadequate where electronic music is concerned. This is because, for the first time, the limits imposed by the construction and use of physical instruments have been removed. At the same time, there may be complications attached to any new form of notation because it will be in the form of "machine language,' i.e., instructions relating to one particular device or system and therefore not common to all methods. Just as an elementary illustration, the information for computer produced music will be totally different from that for a manual system.

Any programming information, to be complete, must include the basic parameters of any musical sound, because unlike conventional instruments a program does not start with a complete tone color but with the separate ingredients. Therefore, any notation of real merit must include means for indicating frequency, intensity, duration, envelope, harmonics, possible noise, and mode of attack and decay (which might be contained in the envelope control.) All of these could have infinite gradations, so clearly a notation must be worked out for the complexity of the system. So, for the time being at least, we can regard any written notation system as temporary and probably unsuitable for many synthesis machines.

All the foregoing values can be represented digitally, but we are faced with a difficulty in regard to time intervals, which must be shown in analog. Nevertheless, the time factor is one of the most important and is related to the envelope and duration factors. One simple way of conveying some of the information in a continuous way is that of the Cologne school of electronic music. This applies to manually operated apparatus, therefore the information (in this example) is limited to the capability of two hands, the intensity being controlled by the foot. Only the frequency, duration and intensity are shown in Fig. 2-3, the reason being that this is the information for one operator, the balance of the parameters either being provided by other operators at the same time, or introduced by rerecording afterwards. All

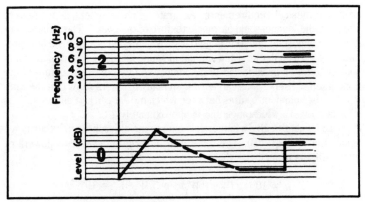

Fig. 2-3. Proposed notation system.

the same, a composer could at least deduce the melodic content from the example, sufficiently extended in time.

In Fig. 2-3 the "2" in the upper stave represents the multiplying factor for the frequencies which are shown in Hz × 100; thus the top line would be 1,000 Hz and the bottom one, 100 Hz; of course, any value can be assigned to the multiplier.

It will be evident later that each system must have its own method of programming, if only for the simple reason that each system is different mechanically and electrically. While, therefore, we have devoted space to the definition of matters like frequency, scaling and tuning, this is merely to provide reference points to which a return can be made as a check. Although if one of the purposes envisaged by the reader is investigation into the properties of conventional musical instruments, then this information will be required.

Before passing to tuning, it might be as well to look at some other parameters of musical sounds. Firstly, *pitch*.

PITCH

Pitch is related to the frequency of a fundamental tone. It is subjective in character; in other words, the assessment of an exact pitch depends on the judgment or acuity of perception of individual persons. The relation to frequency is not a linear function, a pitch interval being representative not of a specific difference, but of a specific ratio of frequencies. The logarithm of the frequency shares with the pitch the property that, on an alteration of the sound by the same pitch interval, it always increases by the same amount, irrespective of the absolute frequency values:

$$\log(f_1/f_2) = \log f_1 - \log f_2$$

A reasonably acute ear can distinguish about one thousand four hundred distinct pitch intervals in fact. Since there are only a hundred and twenty discrete tones in the ET scale, the perception of the ear is much in excess of ordinary musical requirements. Accurate pitch judgment depends very much on the loudness and harmonic texture of the sound. This brings us to the very important question of loudness, which again is a physical interpretation of a particular kind and amount of sound intensity. But this time it is harder to find a basis for accurate comparison within the structure of the tone itself. Observations carried out on many listeners show that the ratio I_2/I_1 of the sound intensities between which the ear can just differentiate is constant over a wide range and is approximately 1·2.

To be able to give a numerical value to the differences in intensity we adopt the decibel (dB). The difference in level between two powers or intensities is n decibels where:

$$n = 10 \log (W_2/10W_1) \quad \text{or} \quad W_2/W_1 = 10^{10/n}$$

If it is remembered that $\log 2 = 0.030$ and that 1 dB corresponds to an energy increase of approximately 25%, the intensity ratio corresponding to a specific number of dB can then be found. Of course, a reference power level must be taken for W_1 above, and this is usually 0 dB = 10^{-16} watts per square centimeter, or 0·0002 dynes per square cm. We therefore show the Fletcher-Munson hearing curves in Fig. 2-4, with the area usefully occupied by music within the range of loudness which the ear can accept. It has already been pointed out that the apparent loudness depends greatly on the complexity or otherwise of the sound; it should be noted that this figure relates to pure or single tones only. If the tones in the region 2000-4000 Hz were complex, they would sound much louder than shown.

A sound cannot be instantly identified; many investigators have examined the time necessary to definitely establish a sense of pitch. There is good agreement regardless of the kind of sound, and it is found that 12 to

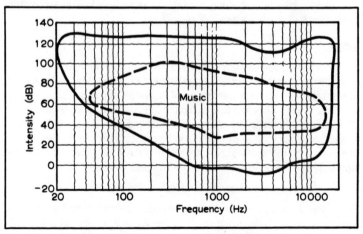

Fig. 2-4. Limits of audibility with music area in center.

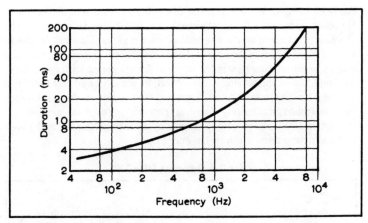

Fig. 2-5. Pitch identification graph.

14 milliseconds is necessary. A shorter period of time induces a sense of irritation, since the ear has a longer resolving time. Figure 2-5 shows the required time against frequency.

It is as well to remember that as we get older, we begin to lose response to the higher frequencies. This is quite marked after some 45 years of age, the effect as measured on a large number of groups of men and women being shown in Fig. 2-6.

TUNING

It is clear that the usual concept of tuning, as applied to a piano, may well not apply at all to electronic tone producers. Nevertheless, they must all have a reference or primary pitch tone, since otherwise it would not be possible to rerecord with other instruments or synthesizers—and little is possible in this art without rerecording. For many years the standard pitch

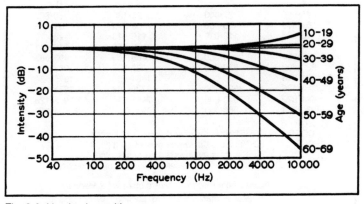

Fig. 2-6. Hearing loss with age.

has been fixed at A = 440 Hz, and this will soon spread to all countries. However, to maintain the tonal virtues of some keyboard instruments, the absolute accuracy of all the intervals is not the same. This may be due to various reasons, but in the case of the piano (where it is most obvious,) the strings really become bars at the upper end, they are so stiff; while at the bass end, the wrapping alters their vibration properties so that there is a kind of 3 tuning system overall. From a synthesis aspect, there is no such thing as a piano pitch merely changing progressively over the compass; the harmonics also undergo great changes, being very prominent at the bass end and nonexistent at the treble end.

Table 2-2. Frequency Table,* Hz.

C	C#	D	D#
16•351	17•323	18•354	19•445
32•703	34•647	36•708	38•890
65•406	69•295	73•416	77•781
130•812	138•591	146•832	155•563
261•625	277•182	293•664	311•126
523•251	554•365	587•329	622•253
1046•502	1108•730	1174•059	1244•507
2093•004	2217•460	2344•318	2489•014
4186•008	4434•920	4698•636	4978•028
8372•016	8869•840	9397•272	9956•056
16744•032			

E	F	F#	G
20•601	21•826	23•124	24•499
41•203	43•653	46•249	48•999
82•406	87•307	92•498	97•998
164•813	174•614	184•997	195•997
329•627	349•228	369•994	391•995
659•255	698•456	739•988	783•991
1318•510	1396•912	1479•976	1567•982
2637•020	2793•824	2959•952	3135•964
5274•040	5587•648	5919•904	6270•928
10548•080	11175•296	11839•808	12541•856

G#	A	A#	B
25•956	27•500	29•135	30•867
51•913	55•000	58•270	61•735
103•826	110•000	116•540	123•470
207•652	220•000	233•081	246•941
415•304	440•000	466•163	493•883
830•609	880•000	932•327	987•766
1661•218	1760•000	1864•654	1975•532
3322•436	3520•000	3729•308	3951•064
6644•872	7040•000	7458•616	7902•128
13289•744	14080•000	14917•232	15804•256

CCCC	16•351 Hz is the lowest note of 32 ft pitch.
CCC	32•703 Hz is the lowest note of 16 ft pitch.
CC	65•406 Hz is the lowest note of 8 ft pitch.
C	261•635 Hz is the so-called middle C of the keyboard.

*Reproduced from *Electronic Music Instrument Manual*,
Sir Isaac Pitman & Sons Ltd, London, 1969.

To conclude the chapter, we give as Table 2-2 a frequency table covering the majority of discrete pitches required for tonal synthesis. This is of course based on the equally tempered scale and does not provide for any stretching or other adjustment of the intervals.

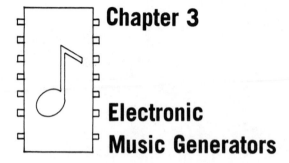

Chapter 3

Electronic
Music Generators

Since there is an infinite variety of musical forms, ranging from the simple melodic line to the most complex orchestration, there must correspondingly be an infinite number of ways or devices for generating the required sound spectrum. Accordingly, we will look first at simple machines, because even with the most elementary apparatus it is possible to rerecord again and again and thus build up a complex spectrum. It is largely a matter of purpose, convenience, skill and cost. The private investigator of limited means need not be at a disadvantage with the university or commercial recording company in this matter. But where the individual may score is in having the facility to imitate any sound regardless of his ability or otherwise to play an instrument, and to be able to set up any combination of sounds at the cost of a few reels of tape. A composer can have copies made for transmission to interested parties, who can then play these back anywhere in the world. How else could this be done except through the medium of electronics?

We know the basic parameters for forming a musical sound; we also know that noise can be a useful adjunct if properly controlled. So let us look at apparatus capable of being constructed at low cost and operated by one person.

INTEGRATED CIRCUITS

It will be noticed that while some of the circuits shown are built up from discrete components, nearly every function required of music generators or their control is available in integrated circuit form, commonly called microcircuits or "chips." The sole purpose of such chips is to bring together, by advanced manufacturing processes, large numbers of circuit elements in one small convenient package. This has really made possible the small portable instruments used by all "groups." As we cannot see inside the chips, it is sometimes not easy to describe their functions in detail, but this can often be deduced from the external components required to complete the circuit—for it is not possible to include items like variable capacitors, potentiometers etc. within the encapsulation. The circuitry needed to connect chips to each other is called interfacing and often consists of discrete components.

The components that surround any one chip to make it work are known as peripherals. We must add that so many new integrated circuits are coming on the market that it is not possible to keep track of all of them. Fortunately, all that are required from a musical aspect are now available.

It should also be made clear that the same kind of chip, for the same duty, may appear under different type numbers from different manufacturers. All IC's terminate in pins which are designed to fit into sockets.

OSCILLATORS

All electronic music producers require pitch or frequency sources. These are oscillators. An oscillator is a device for changing an applied dc potential into an alternating voltage of some designed frequency. At one time these used vacuum tubes, vibrating reeds, photoelectric discs, and magnetic or capacitive rotating elements. Today, these types are obsolete and have been replaced by semiconductor devices. In organs, each oscillator will have a fixed pitch; in synthesizers, the pitch is always variable. The number of possible circuits is legion. We show a number of useful configurations for the beginner, some using discrete components, some with silicon chips. These latter can only be connected in certain ways, of course.

Generally, oscillators can be divided into groups such as keyboard range pitches, A to C (55 to 4186 Hz); low frequency oscillators in the range 1 to 10 Hz, used to supply vibrato, tremolo, or for some other form of modulation or phase shifting; pulse generators, for digital use, synthesizers, percussion, triggering etc.; and noise generators for rhythm units can be included, though they are not strictly oscillators.

Before undertaking any experiments, it must be pointed out that silicon chips are very heat sensitive, and in many cases are influenced by magnetic or electrostatic fields (e.g., rubbing them.) The internal elements are so small they have no resistance to abuse. Always follow the manufacturer's instructions for handling. Transistors are much more tolerant, they are stronger and have wire leads which can be used to conduct away the heat of soldering.

Starting with the simplest circuit (Fig. 3-1,) the two transistors form a two stage direct coupled amplifier. If the collector of TR2 is coupled to the base of TR1 via a blocking capacitor, there will be positive feedback resulting in oscillation. C2 is the timing capacitor and if VR1 (logarithmic) is of good quality, it can provide a very wide range of frequencies. Almost any

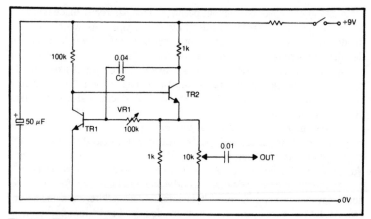

Fig. 3-1. Simple oscillator circuit.

npn transistors can be used, try about 0.04 μF for C2. We can note here that *any* amplifier can be made to oscillate if there is positive feedback from the output to the input.

In Fig. 3-2 we show another kind of useful oscillator, using a unijunction transistor in what is called a relaxation oscillator. The frequency is fixed by C4 and the chain of adjustable resistors, which, though shown as switches, could well be keys of a simple keyboard. The buffer transistor TRs enables a load such as headphones or an amplifier to be connected without affecting the frequency; the gain is low and so is the impedance. The output is of sawtooth shape. There is a refinement here in that a vibrato oscillator is shown on the left; this is a phase shift oscillator working at 6 Hz and can be cut off by S1.

Figure 3-3 is a more modern circuit using voltage control; such a technique permits distant gain control, hum elimination, stepless and noiseless control, and other benefits. The output is a square wave, variable over a wide range by RV1; while the applied vibrato is also variable by RV2. Note that two batteries or a center-tapped supply is required and the center point of this is 0 volts. Many equivalent transistor types can be used.

Figure 3-4 shows the use of an integrated circuit generator (556.) It is a double timer unit of the 555 type, double because we want one-half to act as a vibrato generator. In this case, it is suggested that keys be used as the circuit is quite stable enough to keep in tune for long periods. The pitch frequency is fixed by R1, R2, C1, and the key resistors; the vibrato depth is controlled by VR3. As this timer produces a square wave, and this is not desirable for a vibrato modulator, R4 and C2 filter the square wave to give a smoother effect. It is possible to drive a small loudspeaker directly from this circuit, but to prevent overloading the 556 unit, a 56 ohm resistor is placed in series with the feed capacitor of 100 μF. This circuit may produce strange effects if the smoothing capacitor 0.33 μF is omitted and do not try to force the volume up by increasing the 9 volt supply. This is an example of

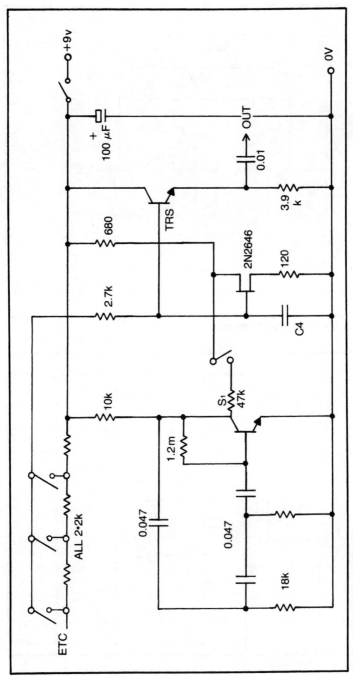

Fig. 3-2. Relaxation oscillator.

31

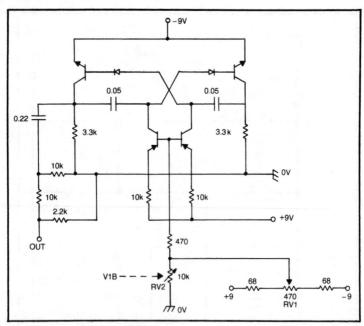

Fig. 3-3. Square-wave oscillator.

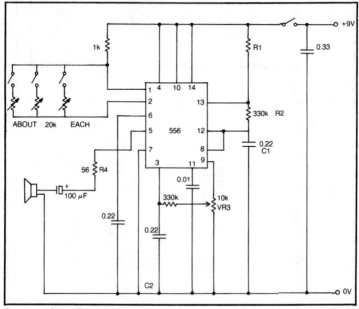

Fig. 3-4. IC oscillator circuit.

32

a chip limitation; if the circuit was replaced by separate transistors, these might blow, leaving the rest of the circuit unharmed; but if the chip is overloaded, the whole thing is destroyed.

We have not really got to the stage of examining waveforms, because this leads to toneforming; basically the sounds from these four circuits are like those from a mouth organ or harmonica. Sometimes waves tend to be rough, especially near the end limits of the controls; any wave, no matter how ragged, can be converted into a perfect square wave by a simple circuit called the Schmitt trigger. It is really a kind of switch which activates very suddenly when TR1 is turned on by a sufficiently high applied voltage. The output jumps to a value which remains at that level until the input voltage drops below the triggering point. However, one can only get a square wave or pulse from this circuit. See Fig. 3-5.

It will be appreciated that operation of any single oscillator system or circuit must result in the production of only one pitch note, though if the device is, for instance, like a multivibrator, the resultant waveforms will be rich in harmonics, which introduce other frequencies. But it is easy to obtain octaves of the fundamental pitch by circuits known as bistable frequency dividers, and these being aperiodic, that is, capable of dividing almost any frequency fed in, can follow gliding tones etc. (Fig. 3-6.) Moreover, the waveform resulting is virtually the same as from the multivibrator and is a substantially square wave.

The bistable is often called a flip-flop, as the switching action jumps from one side to the other; if the output is taken from one collector only, then it requires two input pulses to obtain one output pulse; hence it divides by two. This kind of circuit can be made to oscillate continuously, or give out one pulse and disable itself; such circuits can be seen in various forms later in this book, and an explanation of the circuit is given in Appendix A.

A square wave contains no even harmonics, and if these are called for, the square wave can be converted into an almost linear sawtooth wave, which contains odd and even harmonics in their correct order and amplitude, by means of the circuit shown in Fig. 3-7. Of course, if only fixed frequency intervals are desired, the bistable circuits could be arranged to

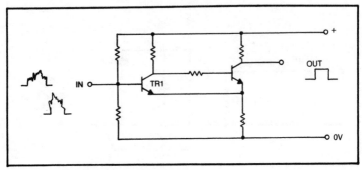

Fig. 3-5. A Schmitt trigger circuit.

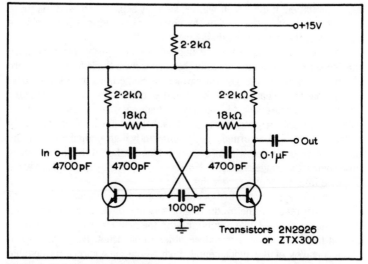

Fig. 3-6. Bistable frequency divider.

divide by some other integer than 2. The use of this kind of circuit means that only one controlling device may be required, since if bistables are connected in cascade, they will automatically turn on and off when the actual oscillators are energized or cut off. Detailed constructional information on this kind of circuit is to be found in most books dealing with electronic organs. Many present day integrated circuits are also available for this purpose, for example, the CD4001 gate. In Fig. 3-8 one section of the gate is used as a buffer, to sharpen up the waveform and minimize the effect of any load on the oscillator. Any unused gates are disabled by strapping their input terminals to the 0V rail. It might be pointed out here that flip-flops, astable, and monostable multivibrators always produce a square wave having a 50/50 duty cycle, i.e., it is symmetrical. This is usual for

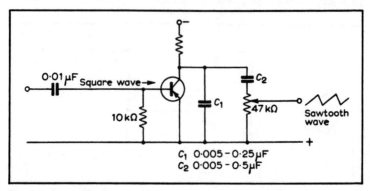

Fig. 3-7. Sawtooth converter.

34

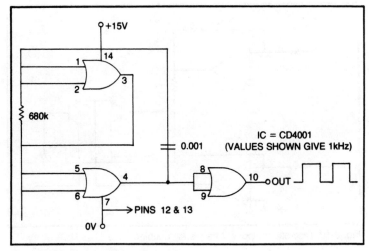

Fig. 3-8. Oscillator using a CD4001.

straightforward musical applications but there are times when the duty cycle could be changed with advantage; until it is brought down to such a long time that only a pulse can appear as in Fig. 3-9 which shows how the circuit of Fig. 3-6 can be made to have a variable mark-space ratio, as it is called, by altering the voltage on the transistors by the variable resistor shown.

Since oscillators and dividers are the prime movers for all electronic musical instruments, we might as well introduce the latest techniques at once, since everything which follows later depends on them. While showing simple oscillators as an introduction, these are not now used to any extent except in certain types of organs, and even there, there is a tendency to seek other methods; but we must always remember the experimenter, who

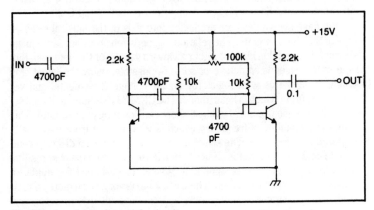

Fig. 3-9. A variable duty cycle circuit.

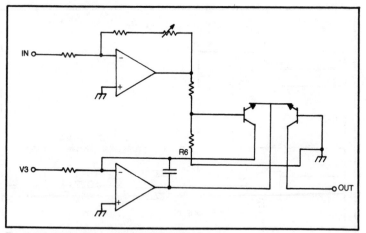

Fig. 3-10. Discrete component frequency doubler.

does not have access to manufacturing processes. Fortunately, he is now able to buy these building blocks for any musical instrument.

KEYBOARDS

If we are going to use a keyboard, then it must be possible to obtain the proper intervals of a semitone since no other kind of keyboard can be played by the human hand. All this is explained in Chapter 2. The keys may span 3, 4, 5 or more octaves but by using frequency dividers one can extend this downwards as far as necessary. It is not satisfactory to generate at low frequencies and multiply upwards. Therefore there is general agreement that one should generate the highest notes which are ever likely to be required. It is not difficult to see that there is no point in going beyond audibility, and as only the 2nd harmonic of top C 2ft pitch (8372.01 Hz) is 16744.03 Hz, this is already beyond average audibility and few speakers will reproduce it. So the highest useful note is that of top C 2ft.

We have shown keys for producing intervals of the musical scale on some of the above circuits. The relationship between notes on, say, a piano is logarithmic and this leads to rather awkward values for the note resistors if the range exceeds an octave or so. It is possible, using the latest chip design, to feed this with linear (or equal) voltage increments, and yet provide an output which is logarithmic. The CEM 3340 is such an IC and so, for a unit increase in control voltage, there is a doubling of the output. This results in a doubling of frequency which is what we get from the equally tempered musical scale. The same effect is obtainable from discrete components, and such a circuit is shown in Fig. 3-10. To obtain the best results, a reference voltage must be applied to V3 and the resistor R6 should be a temperature compensated type. The CEM 3340 is very much more complicated than the simple circuit above, and contains all that is necessary, provided that the control voltages are accurately set.

Even if one intends to use gliding tones or other forms of presentation, it is still necessary to provide the frequency range required. This is where the IC really comes into its own, enabling a series of frequency dividers producing all the lower notes over the whole keyboard to be compressed into a small chip with suitable terminations. Not only are all the notes available, but buffer stages are inserted to isolate different pitches from crosstalk or leakage and the division ratios are permanent and of great accuracy—much closer than one could tune by ear.

TOP OCTAVE DIVIDERS

All the major semiconductor makers produce these top octave dividers, which have to be driven from a high frequency oscillator; any drift in this will be followed through in the divider chains. Perhaps the most popular type is the AY-1-0212A which gives one octave, but the MK 50240 has an extra note, so giving C to C inclusive. It also only needs a single polarity supply line and if the correct driving (or clock) frequency is applied, the division ratios are: 451, 426, 402, 379, 358, 478, 239, 253, 268, 284, 301, 319, and 338. Each output frequency is related to the others by a multiple $12\sqrt{2}$, providing the intervals of the equally tempered scale. See Table 3-1.

As has already been pointed out, these intervals of a semitone cannot be exact with a single divisor; in fact, whatever tuning or division method is used, there will always be small discrepancies. Table 3-1 below gives the exact frequencies from this or other makes of top octave chip, and it will be seen that there is an error for each division; but since there are 1200 cents to the octave, and the maximum discrepancy is 7.5 cents, the tuning is quite adequate to the ear. It is very doubtful if a person could make the tuning closer, that is, with independent oscillators; and this tuning is permanent.

The oscillator frequency for the scale of C would be about 2 MHz and it is interesting to note that the high divisors have to be used to reduce jitter and small notches or pips on the divider waveforms. A useful feature of the single master oscillator is that, since all dividers will follow a change in input frequency, it is easy to re-tune the circuits to play in any key; or even in intervals between recognized key signatures; this is of course an essential feature of synthesizers, where all kinds of glissandos, portamentos and other distortions of the scale are constantly required. The Mostek MK 50240 is in a 16 pin package and must therefore be used with a holder as it is dangerous for the amateur to try to solder it into even a printed circuit board.

This divider chip is of course specially designed to produce properly related notes; if division by only two is called for, there are many chips, usually giving seven stages of two to one division; the CD 4024, 7493, 4016, 5024, etc., are some of the many on the market. There are dividers giving other ratios than two to one, but these have little application for music. These bistables, flip-flops or divide-by-two units naturally follow the chips like the 50240 to give as many lower octaves as required; for one can feed into the next, so constantly lowering the input frequencies; but always by a

Table 3-1. Musical Notes Produced by a Top Octave Divider.

Note	Divide By	Frequency Produced	E.T Frequency	Deviation In Hz
C	239	8372•016	8372•016	—
B	253	7908•742	7902•131	+6•611
A#	268	7466•089	7458•619	+7•470
A	284	7045•464	7039•999	+5.465
G#	301	6647•548	6644•874	+2•674
G	319	6272•451	6271•926	+0•525
F#	338	5919•857	5919•909	−0.052
F	358	5589•139	5587•650	+1•489
E	379	5279•451	5274•040	+5•411
D#	402	4977•393	4978•031	−0•683
D	426	4696•976	4698•635	−1•659
C#	451	4436•612	4434•921	+1•691
C				

divisor of two. In this way, the very lowest notes of an organ are easily reached.

Any frequency source so far described has had a complex waveform. A pure or sine wave is sometimes required. One school of thought is based on the Helmholz premise that any complex tone can be built up with a sufficient number of sine waves, since analysis of any musical sound shows that it is possible to break it down into pure waves. All synthesizers, for example, have sine wave oscillators as well as other kinds. The method of adding sines to form a complex tone is now relegated to research into musical instrument improvements, so that we need only look at some simple "one note at a time oscillators". All circuits produce the purest waveform when they are just on the threshold of oscillation; increasing the power inevitably introduced harmonics.

Probably the best known sine wave circuit is the Hartley, which over the years has taken many forms. As a result of much work, it is possible to extract several different waveforms from a suitable Hartley without any waveforms interfering with another. Such a circuit is shown in Fig. 3-11.

Oscillators using coils and capacitors are more stable than any other kind, if we except those controlled by a crystal. But it is not possible to cover a wide frequency range with a simple control, in fact, the ratio of inductance to capacitance is fairly narrow for any frequency. With the exception of the Allen organ and the Hammond concord, almost every other commercial organ uses the Hartley circuit, or at least one having an inductance for tuning. There is an interesting point here; if the coil is on a ferrite or powdered iron core, then the circuit can be driven hard or made to only just oscillate, with no change in the output waveform if this is taken from the coil. But, if laminations are used for the core, then the oscillator must be driven quite hard to saturate the core. Eddy currents will then flow in the core, and the waveform will have harmonics. In this way (without much distortion of the basic pure wave) small traces of even harmonics can be made to add themselves to the sine wave, and this produces a flute-like tone direct from the oscillator of greater interest than a pure sine wave. In all analog organs, there must be toneforming because they produce ready

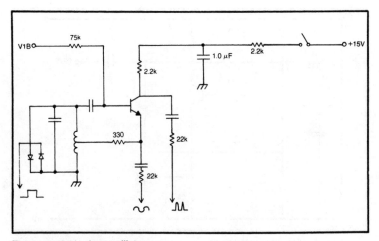

Fig. 3-11. A Hartley oscillator.

built-up waveforms and it is interesting to note that in the Conn and Rodgers organs, laminated cores are used and this forms an easy tuning system by altering the air gap, the laminations being of E and I form.

Integrated circuits can be used for sine oscillators, the complexity depending on the required stability and the frequency range. A good example is given in Fig. 3-12, which uses the ubiquitous 741 amplifier with suitable feedback. The purest sine wave is obtained from the Wien bridge oscillator, shown in Fig. 3-13. Because of the need to alter several circuit elements at once to change the frequency appreciably, it is difficult to cover a range with this bridge. Because the vibrato or tremolo frequency in an

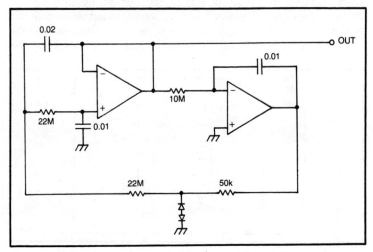

Fig. 3-12. A sine-wave oscillator.

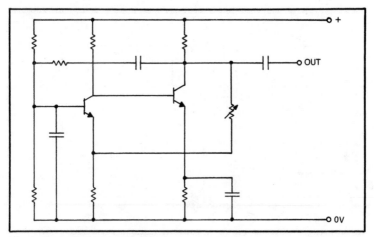

Fig. 3-13. A Wien-bridge oscillator.

electronic organ (for instance) must be sinusoidal to avoid introducing undesirable harmonics into the signal, the Wien bridge in a simplified form like a phase-shift oscillator is almost always used. However, there is at least one circuit in which the frequency is easily and continuously variable by a ganged potentiometer of 10k ohms, and this is shown in Fig. 3-14. The small lamp acts as a kind of barretter or stabilizing agent, holding the amplitude constant. Quite apart from music, this kind of circuit makes a very useful sweep oscillator.

There are many more circuits for pure waves, and with enough filtering, it is possible to get pure waves from almost any other waveform. But, one should steer clear of unnecessary complication. The question of stability has not been raised because it is not always required. Any circuit will hold its tune for a time, but in the case of complex instruments like the organ, it is very important that the tuning should be maintained. Today, the

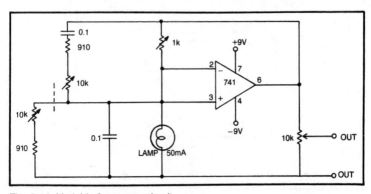

Fig. 3-14. Variable frequency circuit.

tendency is to use one single master oscillator from which all other pitches are obtained by frequency division; but in large organs, and indeed in some polyphonic synthesizers, this system may be multiplied. Now, we find the physical properties of the materials from which the semiconductors are made, beginning to play a part; for no matter how steady the power supplies, with the inevitable temperature rise with time there will be some drift.

Inductive oscillators have a positive temperature coefficient. Capacitors have negative coefficients. It is sometimes possible to get one to neutralize the other; but the properties of capacitor foils, carbon films and other parts of chips like the 555, fight each other to some extent and drift occurs as it does with silicon transistors when warmed. Again it should be stressed that such small changes go unnoticed in single note or melodic instruments; but in multinote devices like organs or pianos, the effect may be irritating. So it is as well to guard against as much of this as we can, and therefore the power supplies should be stabilized. Fortunately, there are now many semiconductor stabilizers which cover most of the requirements. The simplest uses discrete elements, based on the zener diode, which is a diode reversed biased in such a way that a breakdown occurs at a certain voltage. Little current flows above this voltage, and a substantial one below it. The result is that over a wide range of voltage, regulation of the order of ± 2% is possible, given the proper circuit conditions. But the zener can more profitably be used as a constant reference voltage system controlling a power transistor. Large currents can thus be caused to flow in the load. This is the basis of all modern regulators, the majority of which are now encapsulated into chips of more or less complexity. A refinement on the one in Fig. 3-15 is shown in Fig. 3-16, where an amplifying stage is added to the regulator. This compensates for the small change in voltage as the load across the rectifier capacitor increases, because the diode is connected to the emitter of T2 and the base is connected to a proportion of the output voltage. If this latter now falls due to an increase of load, the collector

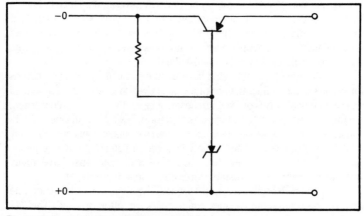

Fig. 3-15. A simple zener voltage regulator.

41

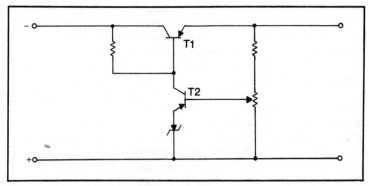

Fig. 3-16. Improved zener voltage regulator.

current will increase because its emitter voltage is held constant by the diode. The base of T1 is connected to the collector of T2n and the voltage of the base rises, therefore, so does the emitter voltage, tending to cancel the original change.

The IC's now available incorporate this and usually, a lot more (temperature compensation, overload protection and other features.) A simple form suitable for the amateur is shown in Fig. 3-17. This provides both positive and negative outputs. A more useful regulator is the type 723, produced by many manufacturers. A circuit for a positive supply is given in Fig. 3-18, giving up to 150 mA. If a negative line is called for, an external power transistor must be connected as in Fig. 3-19, because the reference voltage must be fed back to the inverting input of the regulator, and the output voltage must be fed back to the noninverting input, which is the reverse of the + regulator condition. Most of the chips used for musical purposes require voltages in the range 5 to 15 volts, sometimes positive and sometimes negative with respect to ground. However, many regulators are on the market and the experimenter will have no difficulty in finding what he needs. Just be careful to follow any directions about mounting, heat dissipation and so on. Perhaps it is as well to mention once more that all semiconductor devices are polarity conscious, i.e., they *must* be connected the correct way or they will be destroyed.

Oscillators of a simple kind have been explained above, but whereas for organs these will suffice, because each system gives out well-defined and regular waveforms of fixed pitches; where synthesizers are concerned, we find the need for different circuits of greater flexibility. All synthesizers consist of a number of separate units, so arranged and connected that any combination can be used and rapidly changed. If you are going to produce sounds which have never been heard before, you must have many waveforms, percussion, sustain, filters, envelope controls, etc.

Starting with oscillators, note that stability for any great length of time may not be wanted, so cheaper components can often be used. The 741 amplifier will often be mentioned in these pages, as it is the workhorse of

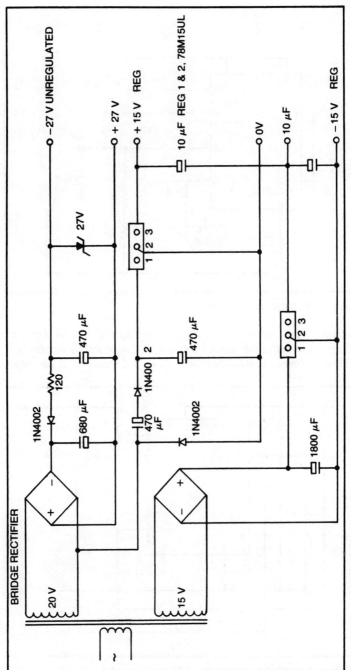

Fig. 3-17. A simple regulator circuit.

43

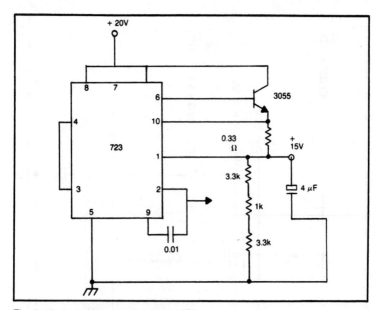

Fig. 3-18. A positive supply using a 723.

electronics and useful for so many purposes. In Fig. 3-20 is a modern
voltage controlled circuit which yields both triangular and square waves. A
field-effect transistor stabilizes the feedback and ensures that the output

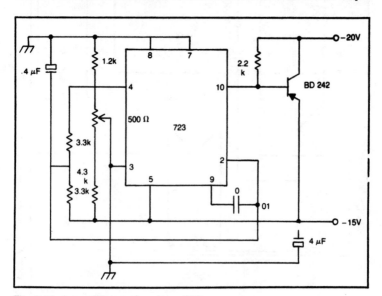

Fig. 3-19. A negative supply using a 723.

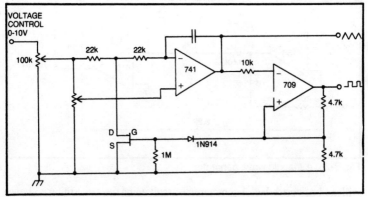

Fig. 3-20. A triangular-wave and square-wave generator.

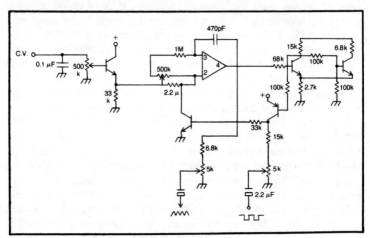

Fig. 3-21. A commercial waveshape generator.

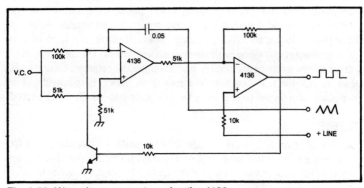

Fig. 3-22. Waveshape generator using the 4136.

45

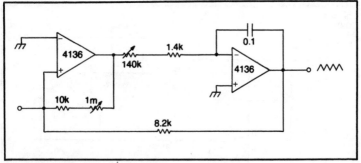

Fig. 3-23. A triangle-wave generator.

will not be overloaded. A commercial circuit doing the same thing is shown in Fig. 3-21, and has adjustments for both waveforms. The 741 is again seen here. Of course, many experimenters will have chips of various kinds in their workshops or dens, so yet another circuit giving the same waveforms is shown in Fig. 3-22. It would hardly be economical to buy the 4136 just for this purpose. It is useful to have both waveforms available from the one circuit, but if only a triangular waveform is required the circuit in Fig. 3-23 is as good as any.

Now the control of frequency in this kind of instrument is nearly always effected by a keyboard using ordinary piano or organ keys. This is where voltage control shows advantages, since it is only necessary to break up the range of resistors across the supply voltage into suitable steps, to give control of semitone or other intervals. A potentiometer or strip resistor can also be used to give gliding tones and long graphited strips are available for this purpose. The waveforms now available (sine, triangular, and square) could be used raw, but nearly always they must be altered to produce a tone color or quality to suit the user. This is done in several ways, but consider steady tones first. These may have an unruly mixture of harmonics, many of which are unwanted. They can be removed or at least modified by filters. Here we have two schools of thought; the need for exact simulation on the one hand; and a more open outlook, where perhaps the sound is to constantly change and does not have to resemble any instrument. Again, we have two outlooks; the "old-fashioned" filters of static low, high, or band pass configuration; along with many resonant filters. On the other hand, active filters using new circuitry may combine the required filtering with gain, so that the insertion loss (common to all filters) is regained and the impedance corrected to suit the kind of circuit into which it is inserted.

FILTERS

Simple filters do three things: lowpass units remove the upper frequencies and pass the lower notes; highpass filters do the reverse; and resonant filters accentuate a part of the applied frequency range to simulate the formants in orchestral instruments.

46

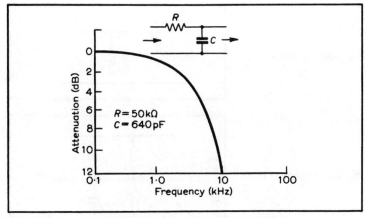

Fig. 3-24. Lowpass *RC* filter; theoretical cut-off $f = 1/(wRC)$.

For the experimenter, quite simple circuits may suffice. In Fig. 3-24 we see a low pass filter, that is, the higher frequencies find it easy to escape to earth through the large capacitors, while the lower frequencies prefer to go through the circuits following. The degree of "smoothing" depends on the ratio of the time constant of the section to the input pulse length. Sections can be cascaded, that is, joined in series, with a progressive improvement in filtering, but with an increase in signal attenuation, as more series resistors are used. This loss can be greatly reduced by replacing the resistors by inductors, as shown in Fig. 3-25. If the resistive loss in the inductors is small, the resonance curve may be steep, in which case the filter will become very frequency selective and many sections of differing values will be required to cover a wide frequency range. It is generally better to arrange such an inductive filter in shunt, as in Fig. 3-26. Naturally, such a circuit is useful for making selected frequencies prominent, for if the efficiency is high enough, the resonant frequency voltage can reach 30 or 40 times the applied voltage.

The circuit which performs the reverse function to Fig. 3-24 is shown at Fig. 3-27. This now prevents low frequencies from passing because the reactance of the very small capacitors is high. Again, for good smoothing there must be more than one section with corresponding losses as shown in Fig. 3-28. Adjustment of all these circuits is by altering one or more of the elements, all of which carry some part of the ac signal, (See Fig. 3-29.) It

Fig. 3-25. Lowpass inductive filter.

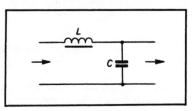

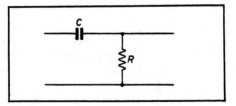

Fig. 3-26. Bandpass filter.

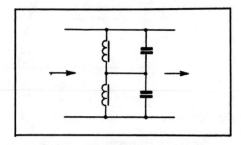

Fig. 3-27. High-pass filter.

would be much more convenient if the characteristics could be controlled progressively and over a wider range. Continuously adjustable filters have been developed many years ago, generally using frequency selective ac networks, a good example being of course the treble and bass controls on modern Hi-Fi stereos. But better control over a wider range is possible by voltage-operated circuits. The frequency selective elements of course remain very much as in any other filter configuration, but the control is quite different.

An example is shown in Fig. 3-30. The signal is applied at A, and the control voltage at B. As the gate voltage of the 2N5163 becomes more negative, the pass band decreases. The overall response can be altered by changing the bridge values at C1, C2, and R1. A simple low-pass active filter is shown at Fig. 3-31 and this opens the way to many experiments. It is more

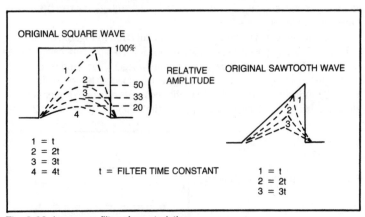

Fig. 3-28. Low-pass filter characteristics.

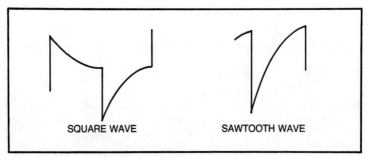

SQUARE WAVE   SAWTOOTH WAVE

Fig. 3-29. High-pass filter characteristics.

usual to extend the filtering action of this circuit by cascading more filter sections as in Fig. 3-32. We shall see an extended example of this type of filter in the organ circuits later on, and if one wants very smooth or flute-like tones over the keyboard compass, this is the way to obtain them from a square wave input. We have already mentioned that it is more difficult to get a good sine wave than a square one, that is why most oscillators produce waveshapes which are far from sinusoidal, it being less costly to correct them afterwards.

Bandpass filters are rarely used in electronic music, they can serve as sharp cutoffs for frequency limiting either at the top or bottom of the range; a circuit illustrating the principle and cutting off at 1 kHz is shown in Fig. 3-33. It will be seen that the 4136 chip is also a very useful device and as square waves have just been mentioned, we show a good square-wave oscillator using this chip in Fig. 3-34. A square wave contains no even harmonics but a very wide range of odd ones, and this is controllable by altering the width of the wave, ranging from a 50/50 period of on to off, to

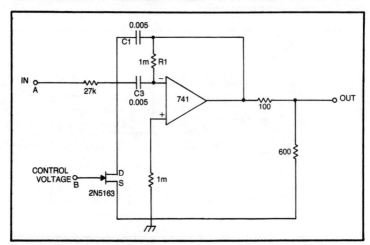

Fig. 3-30. A voltage-controlled filter.

49

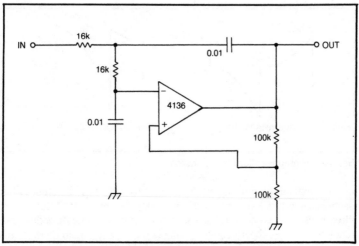

Fig. 3-31. A simple low-pass active filter.

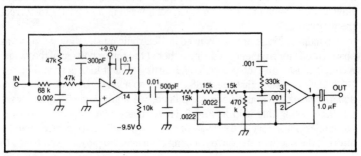

Fig. 3-32. Cascading filter sections.

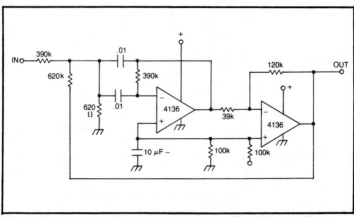

Fig. 3-33. A bandpass filter.

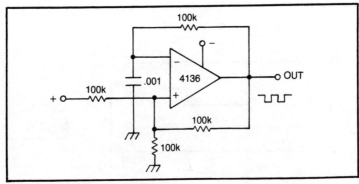

Fig. 3-34. A square-wave oscillator.

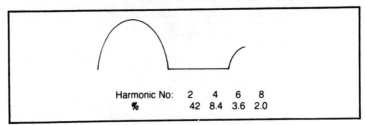

Harmonic No:	2	4	6	8
%	42	8.4	3.6	2.0

Fig. 3-35. Harmonics from a sine wave.

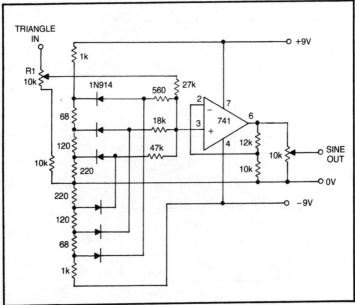

Fig. 3-36. Circuit for converting a triangular wave into a sine wave.

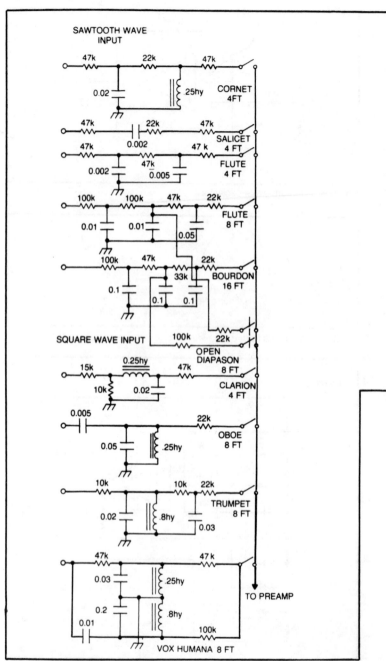

Fig. 3-37. Examples of "old fashioned" static filters.

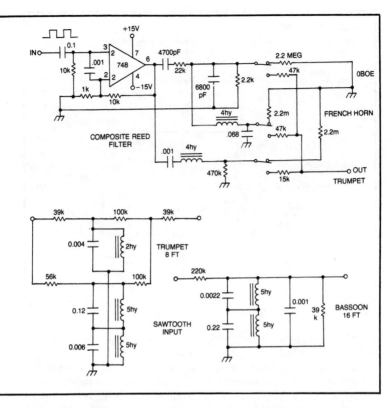

practically an instantaneous pulse like a straight line. These distortions have no real value in music, unless they form part of a digital system of tone generation; and we will come to this presently.

On the other hand, sawtooth or square waves are essential for imitative synthesis, unless digital methods are contemplated. The only operation one can perform on a pure sine wave is to rectify it (apart from attenuating it,) with the result that a small series of harmonics appears (see Fig. 3-35). In an instrument like a synthesizer, where bulk precludes the use of many generators, a sine wave can be produced from a triangular wave, which all such devices possess, by an ingenious circuit as in Fig. 3-36. The assembly of resistors and diodes on the left converts the triangle into a synthetic sine wave by reducing the slope of the triangle in steps as its amplitude increases. One thus gets four steps in every quarter cycle, which is a good approximation to a sine wave; this is amplified as required and R1 adjusts the incoming amplitude to give the best shape to the sine, which in this circuit is symmetrical about 0 volts.

A few of the "old-fashioned" static filters are shown in Fig. 3-37 because these are very effective where bulk and weight are not of importance; and they offer unlimited scope for experiment. All electronic oscil-

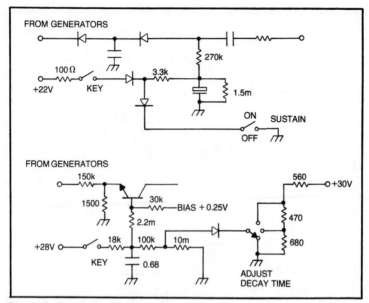

Fig. 3-38. Two simple keyer circuits.

lator systems produce signals which start and stop instantly. This leads to an abrupt effect in the loudspeaker and while useful for aggressive effects, is far from pleasing. So the onset, or attack as it is called, is modified by a form of keying. Today, the signal is rarely keyed directly but rather by some kind of dc control. A common method combines attack control with sustain control, thus satisfying both conditions for a pleasing effect. Two such circuits are shown in Fig. 3-38, the rate of decay being adjustable either by the charging voltage, or the value of the decay capacitor. If the keying "clicks" are not objected to, then plain gold wires can be used; other metals tend to corrode or oxidize with time and produce crackles and scraping noises. The keying circuits mentioned do not alter the overall envelope of the waveform beyond delaying it; for many effects, one may need some modification here—for example, synthesizing a piano or guitar. Envelope shaping circuits tend to be very complex, but one can get good results from the simple arrangement in Fig. 3-39. The applied signal at A is routed through the discharge circuit of the first 748 and then smoothed by the second 748. At the same time, this output is passed through the combined shaper and integrator of the last 748 and gives the choice of a sharp pulse or a trigger waveform for some other circuit—perhaps a piano percussion circuit. A split 9V supply is required for this device, and it must be very well smoothed or a ripple may appear on the decay envelope. It is clear that something between the smooth envelope and the abrupt spike of the pulse is useful in music, and in physical instruments one finds that because of the inertia of the moving parts (even if the moving element is a current of air), instantaneous percussion is almost unknown if one accepts the cymbal or triangle; where because of the force applied, any restraining forces are at once overcome.

Percussive effects are of great value in music. When one considers the paucity of conventional instruments for this purpose, one can see a great many gaps into which all kinds of percussive sounds, both musical and atonal, could fit. Because of the comparatively long resolving time of the ear, there is a limit to the shortness of a percussive signal. It is well known for example that the ear only hears part of the sound of firing a pistol; but for music, times associated with the celeste or glockenspiel are very acceptable. The absolute value of these times are not at all important unless the score calls for this. So one of the most useful percussion circuits is given in Fig. 3-40.

The principle of operation is as follows. The signal to be processed is fed into the two-stage amplifier 602, 603. The amplified signal then passes via the light dependent resistor 412 to the output. 412 is supplied with pulses by the lamp LA1 which is driven by the monostable circuit 405, 406. Negative going pulses are supplied from a manually operated contact driving 403. This circuit normally provides two rates of attack shape, but can be made to run freely at speeds determined by R 574. This produces reiteration, on a sine wave the effect is that of a banjo or mandoline. The performance of the circuit is dependent on the characteristics of the lamp and light dependent resistor, and some experiment may be necessary. Generally a 6 volt 0.04 amp lamp will be suitable. No special kind of contact is required to start this circuit, any kind will do. It should be noted in Fig. 3-40 that the input marked percussion is a contact common to all keys, the

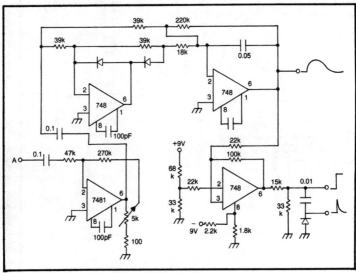

Fig. 3-39. A simple envelope shaping circuit.

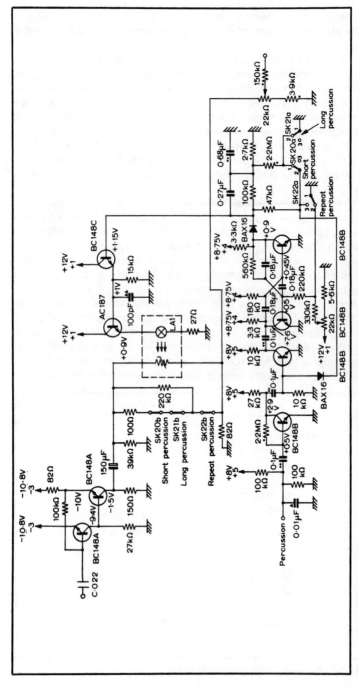

Fig. 3-40. Complete percussion circuit. Symbol ▲ in Figure denotes tolerance: ▲ = 5% ▲▲ = 10%, etc.

other side of which is grounded; and the upper input goes to any signal source.

The advantage of the above circuit is that it is independent of any instrument, and could therefore be used with any tone source. There is little difference between the envelopes produced by the circuit in Fig. 3-40 and the piano envelopes, so it is opportune to show two of the current circuits for this kind of wave shaping. There are piano IC's on the market, but experience shows that somewhat more realistic effects are produced by the following circuits. The distinguishing features are that the volume of sound depends on the rate with which a key is depressed. We have the advantage that by using discrete components, many variants of the circuit are possible to suit different tastes.

A playing key circuit (one of as many as there would be keys on the instrument) is shown in Fig. 3-41. Since no keyboard except a real piano one has the "feel" of mechanical loading, we have to find a way to simulate the inertia of the hammer system. This is done by developing a velocity measuring circuit which in this case is formed by C1, R1, R2, S1, and S2. When a key is depressed, the charge on C1 represents hammer velocity. Transistor TR1 provides isolation between the input and output sections of the circuit and is equivalent to the device in a real piano which allows the hammer to fall back. Capacitor C2 has a charge representing the vibrational energy of a string. D2, S3, and R3 form the damper circuit, which can be disabled to give a sustain action. Diode D1 blocks the pitch signal when the circuit is not active. The discharge times of the C2's vary to imitate the longer time required for the bass notes to die away. If a key is pressed very quickly, the capacitor C1 only loses a volt or two, so that almost 5 volts

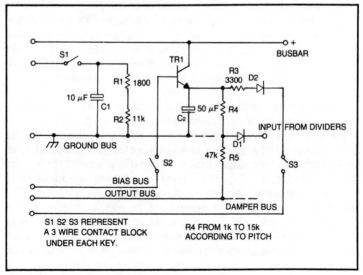

Fig. 3-41. A playing key circuit.

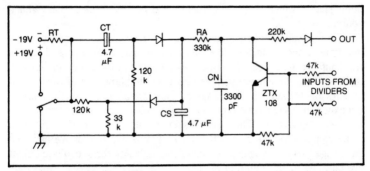

Fig. 3-42. A simple piano circuit.

appears on C2; but if the key is pressed only lightly, then C1 discharges almost to the bias voltage (0.7V,) so that a very small charge appears on C2.

Another very successful piano circuit is shown in Fig. 3-42. Again, it is only the touch characteristics which interest us. The key switch is normally at ground potential until a note is played, the voltage across capacitor CT is then zero. When a key is pressed, the contact leaves the ground busbar and starts to travel towards the 19V busbar. This allows capacitor, CT to charge through resistors RT, the voltage following the time constant RT CT to the final level of approximately 17V. When the key completes its travel, a 19V pulse is applied to CT which raises the voltage at the junction of CT and RT gy an amount equal to 19V minus the voltage across CT at that time. As the key travel times are around 2 ms to 40 ms, there will be a variable attack voltage passed to the decay circuit. This is applied to the capacitor CS through the diode, which charges to a level determined by the ratio of CS to CT, followed by a quick decay to a level of 3V (plus the forward volt drop of the diode.) There are different values of the components to give a variation in decay time over the compass. Perhaps we should explain that the expression "compass" means the number of notes which can be played, it may cover 3, 4, 5 or more octaves or be an odd number of notes; e.g., a piano is often of 7¼ octaves compass. (An octave, of course, is 12 notes.)

There are other attributes of musical sounds which are very important. No tune can have any impact unless it has rhythm; indeed, it is certain that before there was any music as we know it, there were drums and other rhythm sources. Today there are microchips like the M252 and M253 which incorporate the whole of the circuitry required to produce eight or more rhythms as indicated in Fig. 3-43. The external elements are few as can be seen, the variable clock generator enables one to set the rate of beat. The expression "clock" here is in general use for oscillators driving some counting device, and has nothing to do with a timepiece. The experimenter can make up any or all of the circuits used in these chips, in a very simple way and at little cost; all kinds of different rhythms and different pitches for sounds like drums or cymbals can be tried, in the chips these have fixed values. A selection of such circuits are shown in Figs. 3-44 through 3-52.

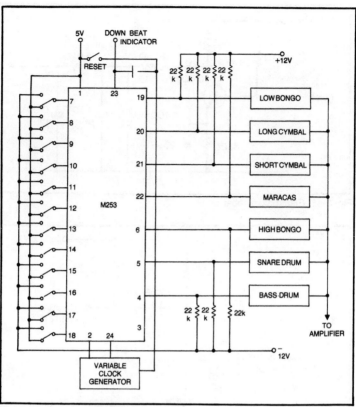

Fig. 3-43. A rhythm generator circuit.

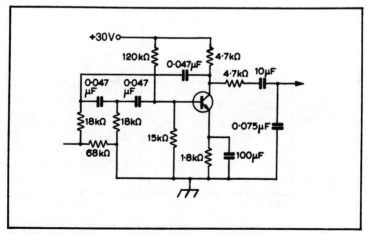

Fig. 3-44. Electronic drum beat oscillator.

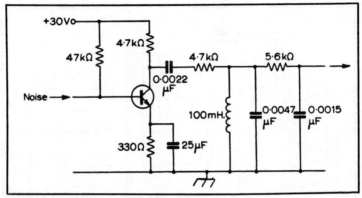

Fig. 3-45. Electronic cymbal circuit.

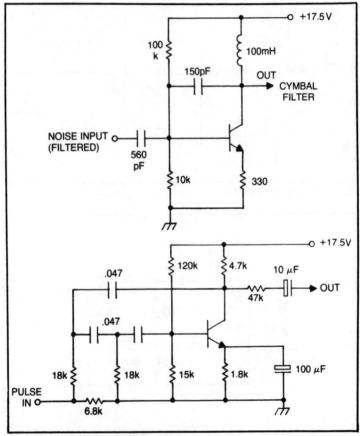

Fig. 3-46. A drum generator circuit.

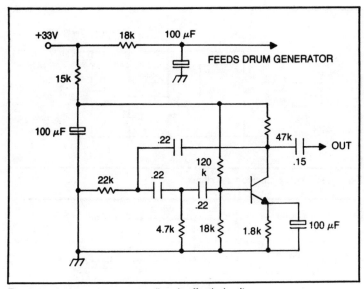

Fig. 3-47. A shimmer generator (brush effect) circuit.

We see from the foregoing that noise generated electrically is used for any sudden sound like drums, cymbals etc. One can use a selected zener diode, a diode over-run, or a transistor with the collector cut off; this is the method used by most manufacturers. We show a selection of noise generators in Fig. 3-53, from which it will be seen that they are all very

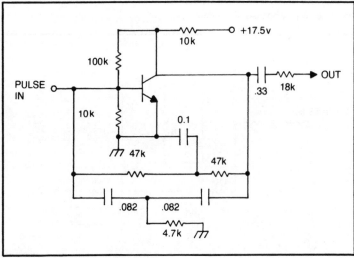

Fig. 3-48. A bass drum filter circuit.

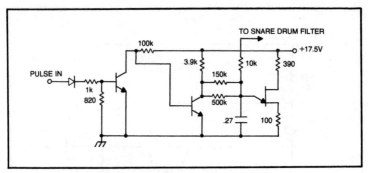

Fig. 3-49. A snare roll oscillator circuit.

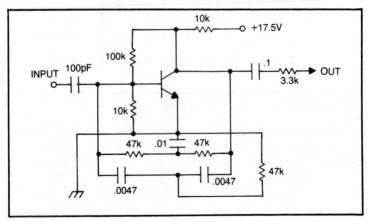

Fig. 3-50. A snare noise filter circuit.

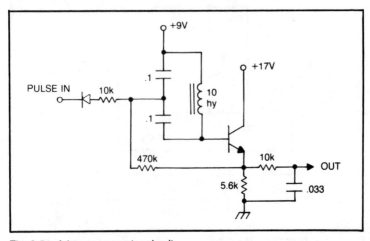

Fig. 3-51. A bongo generator circuit.

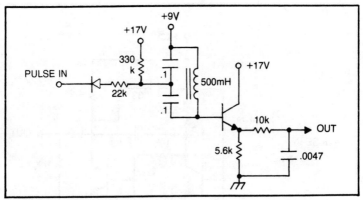

Fig. 3-52. A block sound generator circuit.

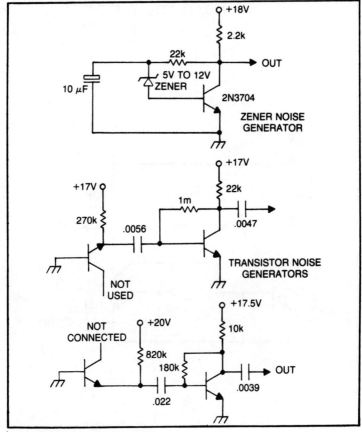

Fig. 3-53. Noise generator circuits.

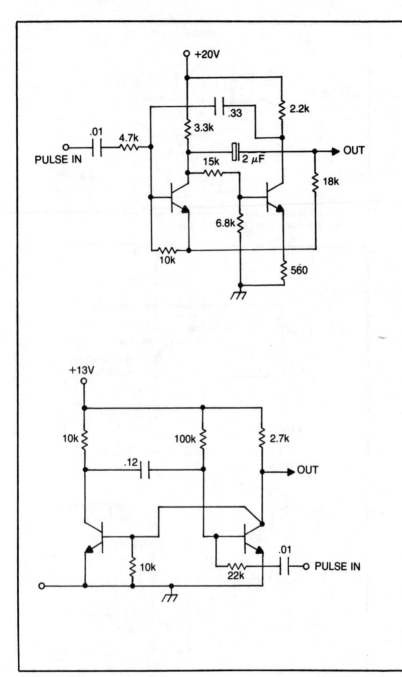

Fig. 3-54. One shot multivibrators.

64

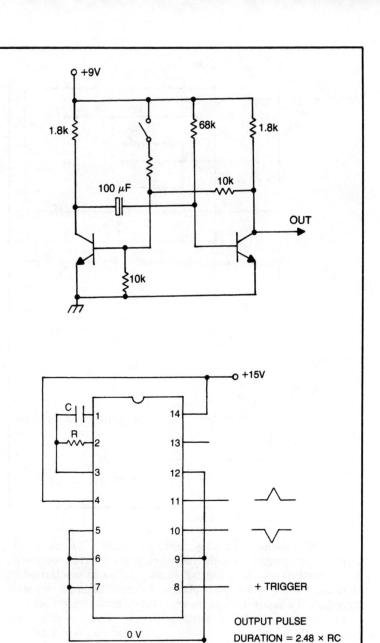

+9V

1.8k

68k

1.8k

100 μF

10k

OUT

10k

+15V

C 1

14

R 2

13

3

12

4

11

5

10

6

9

7

8 + TRIGGER

0 V

OUTPUT PULSE
DURATION = 2.48 × RC

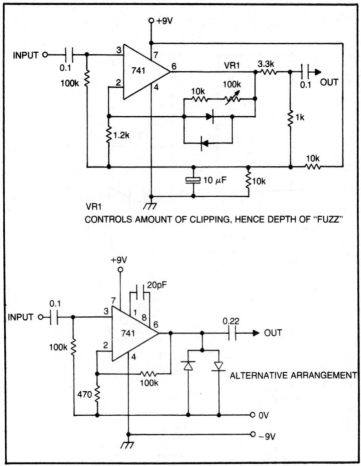

Fig. 3-55. Simple "fuzz" effect circuits.

similar. One has only to find a noisy transistor to succeed. The noise covers a wide frequency spectrum so that for high pitched sounds like the cymbal, the low fractions must be filtered out. Equally, the low content is required for bass drums and the like. Many of these rhythm sounds are of very short duration, so it is usual to activate the appropriate shaping circuits from a one shot multivibrator, which is an oscillator which gives only one pulse, then cuts itself off until re-biased by a switch, key or automatically by some form of electronic gate (Fig. 3-54.)

Most of the devices so far examined are free from distortion; but some musical effects call for this treatment and are associated with "group" playing. It is found easier to start with a real instrument which can quickly revert to normal tone and pitch, than to synthesize these effects; the most

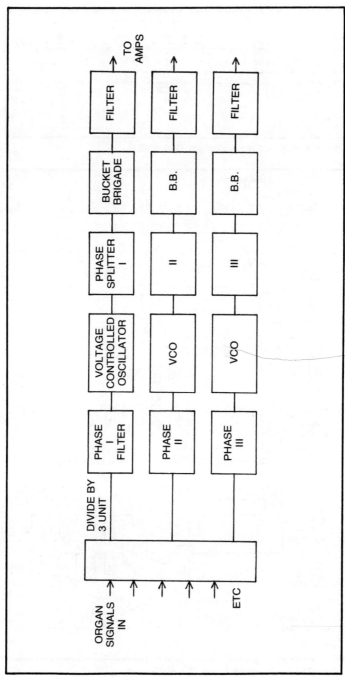

Fig. 3-58. A block diagram of a bucket brigade IC.

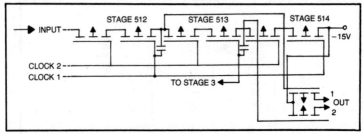

Fig. 3-59. A simplified drawing of the TDA 1022.

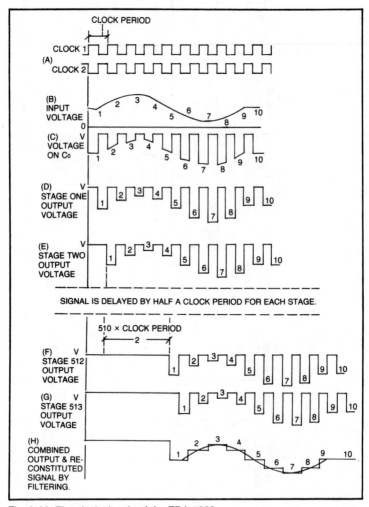

Fig. 3-60. The clock signals of the TDA 1022.

nalities like strings. Only the vco's and the bucket brigade devices (TDA 1022) are encapsulated, so a great deal of adjustment and variation is possible with the discrete components around the other parts of the circuit (Fig. 3-58.)

As the TDA 1022 is such a widely used component, we give a few details about it. There are 512 delay stages, plus one or two correcting gates. In Fig. 3-59 a few of the gates and the inputs for signal and clock circuits are shown. The delay for the whole line is 3.5 ms using a clock frequency of about 100 Hz. The input signal level should not exceed 2V to keep distortion low, and there will be a little attenuation over the system. The clock signals are produced in opposite phase and the progression of the system can be followed in Fig. 3-60. The relative position of the delayed final signal can be seen. We show this with a sine wave (which would not be so in practice) but the true spectrum of a complex wave would be far too complicated to show on a small scale and would obscure the analysis of the device. A suitable active filter for the TDA unit is shown in Fig. 3-61.

A circuit device which has many uses but seems to be rather out of fashion at the moment, is the ring modulator. This forms a useful means of superimposing a recorded pattern of noise, rhythm, blanking pauses, etc., on sounds passing through the modulator. In essence, we have a signal source, a suitable carrier frequency (above audibility) and a tape player containing pulses as required to form some pattern. The tape is connected to the input terminals of the ring modulator, which will only pass the sound when the carrier and signal frequency are applied simultaneously. The modulator has considerable stop-band attenuation against individually occurring frequencies. Now, if a series of pulses is applied to the tape loop in accordance with the desired rhythmic structure, the modulator will be blocked against the musical sound wherever the tape is free of impulses. In

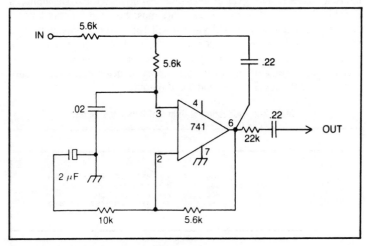

Fig. 3-61. An active filter for the TDA 1022.

71

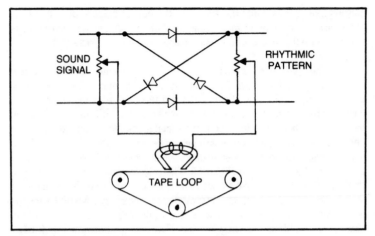

Fig. 3-62. A ring modulator.

this way, a desired rhythmic pattern can be imposed on the sound. It is only necessary to make sure that the resulting products of modulation lie above the range of hearing (30 kHz has been used successfully.) See Fig. 3-62. Again quite new combinations of sound can be made to appear because if various frequencies are simultaneously injected, new sounds are made.

These new sounds are the result of adding and subtracting the input frequencies, giving sum and difference frequencies which only rarely relate harmonically to the original frequencies. By beating two of the internal oscillator frequencies together as shown, then as the variable frequency unit is gradually changed in pitch towards a lower octave, the two sum and difference tones resulting can be heard, one rising in pitch and one falling, as in Table 3-2. Note that sine waves only must be used for this kind of treatment, complex waves will yield results of a very confusing nature, incapable of analysis. After processing in the modulator, resultant signals can be shaped, filtered, or otherwise manipulated to give endless effects. Because the modulator responds to most frequencies equally, the only control is for the level of the modulated output.

Table 3-2. Production of Sum and Difference Tones.

Falling										
Sums	600	580	560	540	520	500	480	460	450	*Heard*
Oscillator 1	300	280	260	240	220	200	180	160	150	*Suppressed*
Oscillator 2	300	300	300	300	300	300	300	300	300	
Difference	0	20	40	60	80	100	120	140	150	*Heard*
Rising										

REVERBERATION

One of the essential ingredients of most music is reverberation or, in extreme cases, echo. In a normal room which is not cubic or round, the path lengths from a fixed sound source vary in length to an observer also fixed in some other part of the room. Therefore, the sound must take longer or shorter times to return to the listener if the room is rectangular. All this time, energy is being lost from the initial sound source, partly by absorption by walls, clothing, etc., and partly by sheer distance. Some is also lost by repeated reflections from hard objects like windows. That is why one never finds windows in recording studios.

In a domestic room of average size, it is unlikely that any path length for reflected sound will be long enough to give an appreciable delay; sound travels at about 1200 feet per second. So some means must be found to simulate the reflections which color the sound so agreeably. Reverberation varies with frequency, power, and distance, therefore one can never exactly imitate the acoustic effect of a large room or hall. Also, most artificial systems have resonances or restricted frequency ranges. Quite often the effect is extended to sound like echo, and this is easy electrically and instantly controllable, which is an impossibility with any acoustic surroundings.

We now come to reverberation. This property, occuring naturally in large auditoriums or halls, can be simulated in several ways. Artificial reverberation is usually introduced by magnetic systems employing tape

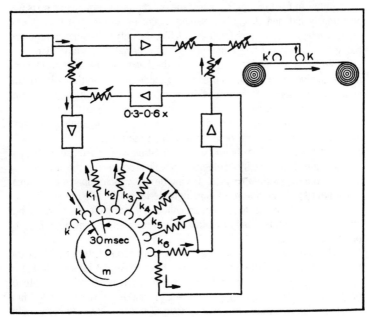

Fig. 3-63. Reverberation by magnetic loop tape.

loops or magnetic drums, because there is no real storage time at normal tape speeds, the signal being erased as soon as it has passed through the device. If we look at Fig. 3-63, it will be seen that the signal is fed to a recording head k_1 which is preceded by an erase head k_r. Additional recording heads k_2 to k_6 are spaced out at distances to give successive delays, easily calculated from the known tape speed or rate of drum rotation. Because the head spacing must not be so great as to give the impression of a number of separate signals, the total delay cannot be sufficient for a great many purposes; therefore, a feedback circuit is used as shown in the diagram, whereby some of the output from selected heads is returned and superimposed on the input. This will result in another series of six weaker but further delayed signals in the output, and indeed it is possible to do this once more so that, in fact, if the original delay was 180 milliseconds, the second feedback would extend this to 360 ms, and the final extension would produce 540 ms, which is a good value for many purposes. There is, of course, no reason why signals should not be supplied to a loudspeaker from the music tapes, fed to a long period echo chamber, then picked up by microphones and returned to the tapes.

Mechanically, it is easiest to use a loop of tape, perhaps 3 ft long, of which some 12-18 inches would embrace a brass drum having a very accurately machined face and bearings. Spring loaded rollers hold the tape to the drum face and the heads are lightly in contact when required. The heads are accurately ground to the drum contour, but the ratio of diameters is usually great so the friction is very small. Electrically, there is a limit to the number of feedback paths, since the overall frequency response is not completely flat and this progressively becomes worse. Small magnetic delay machines are commercially available, the only maintenance required being the cleaning of heads and occasional renewal of the tape loop. It is possible, in some designs, to position the heads on the smooth or non-magnetic side of the tape, so preventing oxide pickup on the poles of the head; the increased separation, which results in loss of some high frequencies, can be compensated for either by top note "boost" or by much narrower head pole gaps, since there is now no risk of clogging of the gaps, and a cleaning device can be used to rub on the tape.

Another method of obtaining reverberation is to make use of a transmission line. This is really an electromechanical converter, the signal being applied to a magnetic or crystal driving device which imparts a torsional movement to a coiled wire of considerable length. It is quite possible to calculate any delay, absorption or transmission factor for these wires, but since they are quite easily obtainable on the open market, it is best to purchase as required.

The rate of propagation in a wire is a function of its length and the transmission rate of the material itself; the wire might be straight but is more conveniently in coiled form, to take up less space. The rate of propagation is the same for all frequencies, and if the wire is coiled in a constant-diameter helix, this will be true. But if the diameter of the helix were to vary, the rates of transmission would also vary as the mean length

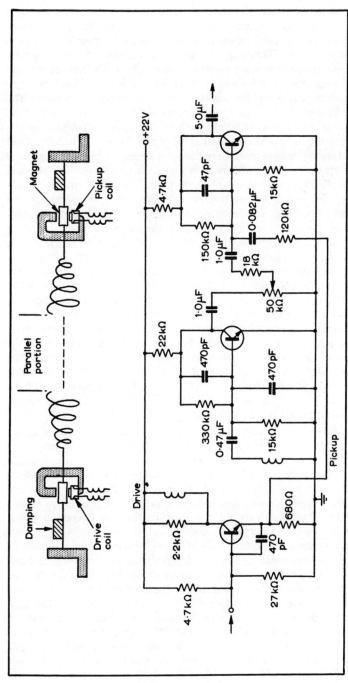

Fig. 3-64. Taper spring reverberator and drive amplifier.

of the turn. In this way it is possible to obtain delays which obey some law in relation to frequency, which is the natural function. On the other hand, multiple springs can be made to produce many phase relationships which produce curious fluttering reverberations because of this constantly changing phase. The music signal is applied to the wire via an amplifier and recovered from the other end by a transducer. It is then either used on its own or combined with the original signal in any desired proportions. The overall design of the system will determine the time in toto, some of the signal being of course reflected a number of times to and fro with continually decreasing energy. A diagram of one method can be seen in Fig. 3-64. There must always be some means of regulating the energy delivered to the line to prevent overloading, and quite often it is necessary to have filter circuits to limit the frequency range applied; obviously large low-frequency signals would seriously disturb the line. For this kind of work, a conventional echo chamber would be more desirable. Other devices are possible. A thin sheet of steel can be driven at one corner with a pickup at the diagonal opposite (the sheet being suspended by a cord.) The RCA delay line can be used. It consists of a long coiled tube, 100 feet or more, with thin ribbon microphones introduced at intervals to give multiple time delays, (the whole being fed back again and again, to simulate the multiple reflections occuring in any large room or building.) The tube was driven by a moving coil speaker element at one end and the other end was plugged with a non-resonant substance, (for example, cotton wool.) If the reverberation is excessive, some peculiar effects are possible. For instance, if white noise (that is, the whole of the noise spectrum generated by a noise transistor) is overlaid by a tune played on simple sine waves, an ethereal sound appears, like that made by wind in telegraph wires, or the Jews Harp. It is also possible, with the tape loops, to pick off at each head and so produce reiteration as may be commonly heard in TV programs.

Purely electronic reverberation is also possible by means of bucket brigade chips. The delay per unit is quite small, but as many required can be cascaded (one commercial unit uses 12 in series.) They have the advantage that there is no appreciable peaks or resonances, but they are easily overloaded. Indeed, this is one of the great disadvantages of all the devices on the market, all can cause distortion and for that reason, are usually shunted across only part of the signal path, the main frequencies going through the power amplifiers directly.

An extremely important attribute of electronic music is vibrato or tremolo. The former type of modulation affects both amplitude and frequency, the latter amplitude only. Both have their uses and both can be used at the same time in the one instrument. These effects came into being with the electronic organ, the rather lifeless tones of which (in the earlier days) required this auxiliary assistance. There are many circuits of this kind, the essence of these devices is that they should supply a sine wave, which acts as a carrier for the main tones. Any harmonics introduced would seriously distort the signal from the generators. The Wien bridge mentioned earlier is a good choice, but more costly to make than the simple phase-shift circuit

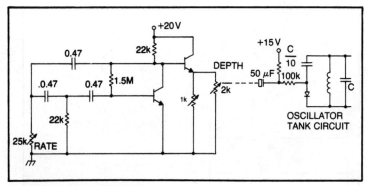

Fig. 3-65. A phase-shift circuit.

of Fig. 3-65. This will function well and the usual practice has been to apply the modulation directly to the oscillators. It is possible to have many vibratos connected to a complex generator system like an organ, but one must ensure that this extra circuitry, when not in use, does not alter the tuning or load the oscillatory circuits.

A better approach is to combine vibrato, tremolo and a certain degree of phase shifting in one unit, and this can be done with the aid of photoelectric devices which operate with no discontinuity of the circuit and have a nice inherent time delay which gives realism. The circuit acts as a static phase shifter when the lamps are not lit, that is, when the oscillator is turned off. The lamps are shown separately from the photocells for clarity, in reality they can be bought encapsulated together and so form an automatic light-tight enclosure. In Fig. 3-66 the units have three photoresistors and one 6 volt lamp in the one package. All transistor are type 2N3565 or equivalent. In the case of organs, it is popular to have mechanical modulators like the rotating Leslie systems; but they are not applicable to portable apparatus and, not being electronic, are not described here. There are electronic simulators, but they do not give the effect of sound being swept round a room of unsymmetrical dimensions and have not attained the popularity of the rotating curtains of the Leslie system.

Organs raise special problems. Basically sustained tone instruments, such sounds are very susceptible to the slightest interference, especially clicks and hum. Probably the main interest centers around the methods of keying the signals. We have already touched on this matter, but now there are chips which combine frequency division with keyers giving click-free results and sometimes combining buffer transistors or protection against short circuits. Such a unit is the TD 1008, capable of combining keying, percussion, decay, staircase-wave formation, and other functions all in the one chip. Figure 3-67 illustrates the connections from this device which requires a square wave to drive it. Five octavely-related tones appear at pins 2 to 6, and note that because the square wave is symmetrical about the mean dc level, there can be no click or thump from keying the signal. Figure

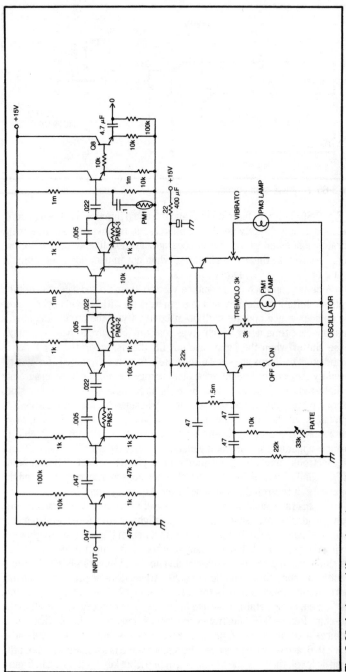

Fig. 3-66. A phase-shifter using photoresistors.

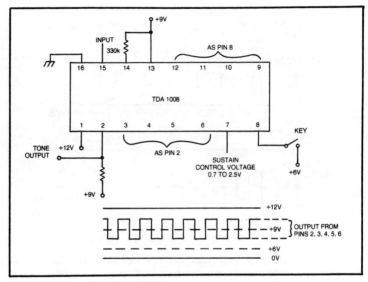

Fig. 3-67. TDA 1008 connections.

3-68 illustrates a complete attack and decay circuit attached to the TDA. As the voltage on pin 7 is increased, the key impedance is reduced, which shortens the sustain period. The resistor in series with the key contact prevents any possible sparking at the contact (due to the discharge of C1,) and introduces an intial slow attack in the amplitude of the note when a key is depressed. A fast attack is possible if C1 is reduced in value, but keep R1 at 10k. The range of decay possible from Fig. 3-68 is shown in Fig. 3-69. The actual shape of the decay is the lower sketch; this is the maximum effect, obtained by reducing the value of R2.

The reverse condition, a sharp percussive attack, is possible with this

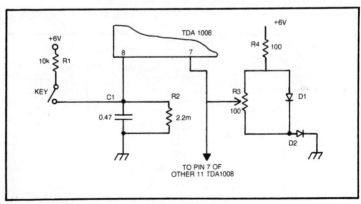

Fig. 3-68. Slow attack and adjustable decay circuit.

79

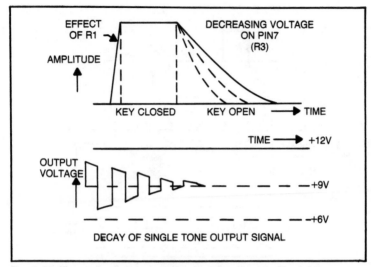

Fig. 3-69. The range of decay possible from the circuit in Fig. 3-68.

unit if a simple charging circuit is added as in Fig. 3-70. A back stop contact wire is required as shown, so that, when the key is at rest, capacitor C1 is charged through R1 and discharged through R1 and R2. When the key is released, the voltage is removed from the input, and the output signal will stop suddenly. In fact, all three functions, percussion, attack, and decay could be combined in one circuit using a three gang switch as in Fig. 3-71. In a practical organ system, it would be necessary to select the values of the resistors and capacitors to get the best compromise of the "percussion with sustain" effect.

An interesting application is the coupling of fifths to fundamental pitch notes. This is done in pipe organs to obtain a synthetic 32 ft pedal bass, often labeled resultant 32 ft. For example, bottom C 16 ft and the G above are coupled to sound together. But we find the interval of a 5th on manuals as

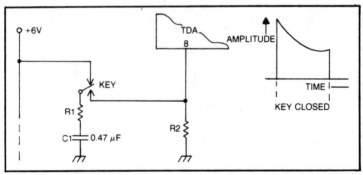

Fig. 3-70. A simple charging circuit.

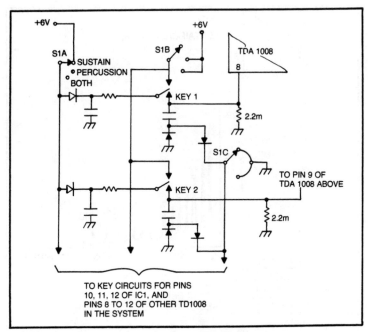

Fig. 3-71. Combining percussion, attack, and decay.

well, and with this chip we save busbars and perhaps extra contacts; of course, thirds or any other intervals could just as well be selected. The diodes prevent selection backwards, so to speak. See Fig. 3-72.

Adequate tonal synthesis in a conventional electronic organ requires both square and sawtooth waveforms at the inputs to the tone forming

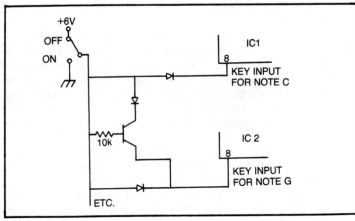

Fig. 3-72. A simple "percussion with sustain" circuit.

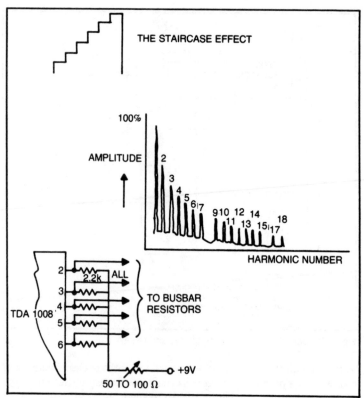

Fig. 3-73. Converting square waves into sawtooth waves.

circuits. With the TDA 1008, the output waveforms are square. They can be converted into sawtooth by addition in the manner of Fig. 3-73. Resistors from each octave are summed on a busbar and produce a composite waveform like that in the figure. The square wave has only odd harmonics, the "staircase" wave contains even ones as well. The sawtooth is not quite regular in shape, but as can be seen from the harmonic analysis, they are all there—at least, quite sufficient for excellent toneforming. By short circuiting the resistor in the positive lead, square waves are available. The M108 IC is even more versatile, as it not only contains the dividers and buffers, but also a complete rhythm device; the above description should suffice to understand its functions.

We have so far examined electronic tone production by conventional or analog methods. In this case, the intervals of the octave are fixed by the tuning and octave relationships cannot be varied. With digital circuits, the ratios between the frequencies of the 12 notes of the octave can be fixed by the design of the circuit. A major difficulty is that the ratios corresponding to the equally-tempered scale are irrational ones, as we have seen in

Chapter 2. This means that they can only be approximated, but this has to be very close to obtain a result acceptable to the ear. It should not be more than 0.05% of the true frequency. The reason for this is that the interval of the fifth in the ET scale is only 0.1% smaller than the true fifth (1.4983 instead of 1.5000.) If the frequency error is greater than 0.05%, two notes forming a fifth can be wrong by 0.05% in different directions, so that the interval may become equal to a true fifth, or larger. Then not all the fifths are smaller than the true fifth and this degrades the tuning.

BINARY NUMBERS

Most designers approximate the twelve tone frequencies by dividing a single high master frequency by twelve carefully chosen large integers (between 200 and 300, as we have seen.) In this way, a train of pulses is obtained with a number of pulses per second that approximates to the required frequency. However, provided that the timing error for the separate pulses does not exceed a few percent of their average spacing, trains of pulses that are not absolutely periodic are heard as a single tone. The pitch corresponds to the average repetition rate and if the aperiodicity is limited to a few tenths of 1%, the small noise—like signal resulting due to this is hardly noticeable. The tolerance of the human ear allows us to assemble the required number of pulses per second by adding trains of pulses at differing repetition rates. The pulses are derived from a master oscillator by progressive frequency division. For simplicity it is easiest to show all frequencies in the binary system, normalizing half the master frequency to 1. The master frequency, its octave, then would have the frequency 10 in binary notation, and all twelve notes within the octave can be given by a binary number between 1 and 10. See the Table 3-3. The pulse trains obtained by further halving correspond with the binary numbers 0.1, 0.01, 0.001, etc. If the frequency x is made to correspond to the note C, then the A (for example) of the ET scale is given by 1.1010111010, formed by adding the

Table 3-3. Scale of Equal Temperament.

Note	Decimal	Binary
C	2·0000	10·0000000000
B	1·8878	1·1110001101
A#	1·7818	1·1100100001
A	1·6818	1·1010111010
G#	1·5874	1·1001011010
G	1·4983	1·0111111110
F#	1·4142	1·0110101000
F	1·3348	1·0101010111
E	1·2599	1·0100001010
D#	1·1892	1·0011000010
D	1·1225	1·0001111101
C#	1·0595	1·0000111101
C	1·0000	1·0000000000

Fig. 3-74. Forming a note by adding pulse trains.

```
1
0.1
0.001
0.00001
0.000001
0.0000001
0.00000001
_____
1.10101101
```

following pulse trains (Fig. 3-74.) The other notes are formed in the same way. The number of binary digits required is determined by the accuracy to which the binary synthesis frequencies have to match the frequencies required by the system of tuning. If the deviation is to be no greater than 0.05%, then this is 1/2000 which means an accuracy of $1/2^{11} = 1/2048$ for the binary frequencies, so we need eleven digit binary numbers, i.e., eleven frequency dividers.

The aperiodicity of the pulses so obtained is too great to allow them to be used directly as tones for a musical instrument, so the pulses are used alternately. The position is then improved by a factor of two, for the timing error remains the same while the average period is now twice as long. This procedure is carried out at high frequencies and the sum frequencies so obtained are divided by a large number. For example, if a master frequency of 2 MHz is used, the large number would be $2^9 = 512$. This would give the highest octave to be used. The lower ones are then divided down in the usual way to give the raw tones, which are treated by filters as required. In this system (Philips) the pulse trains in different rows never coincide. Similar results can be obtained by suppressing a number of pulses from the master oscillator, i.e., by subtraction instead of addition. Although the system is complicated when completed, by use of the latest encapsulation methods, a complete organ generator covering 9 octaves can be produced on a printed board only 4½″ × 4″ × ¾″. The outputs are square waves, perfectly shaped. To assist others thinking in terms of binary construction of waveforms for organ purposes, we give the decimal and binary equivalents for the next octave down, from which the notation for all other octaves can be worked out.

There are some exotic IC's for non-musical use and for auxiliary purposes with tone generators, like the Texas 76477 effects generator, which is primarily designed for video games but can be used to provide swishing kinds of noise and contains a super low frequency oscillator whose range starts far below audibility and so can be used for effects like drums or wind noises, or for modulation of phase shifters to give moaning or other weird sounds. The CD4046A phase-locked loop has applications as a voltage to frequency converter or for frequency synthesis and since it contains its own voltage controlled oscillator, it can enable frequency dividers connected between pins 3 and 4 to supply signals to the two phase comparators which, when smoothed by the filter, can drive the vco so that modulation takes place between control voltages applied to R1 and/or R2, and complex pulses emerge from pin 1. These and the pulses from pins 2 and 13 can be used to modulate synthesizer tones and to make them appear to advance and recede, giving "presence" to the sounds. Figure 3-75 shows the unit.

Another application of the CD4046A or the LM565 is to hold an externally generated frequency constant by means of the phase-sensitive detector. This is compared to the frequency generated in the internal oscillator, and a voltage output obtained from the phase-sensitive detector. If this is not too far removed from the input frequency, the voltage from the phase sensitive unit can then be used to correct the injected frequency until the two are the same and of the same phase. A device of this kind is used in the Allen digital organs to hold the generated frequencies to the limits required for music.

There seems to be some difficulty in playing only one note at a time on the foot pedals of electronic organs; doubtless this is due to the abbreviated and non-standard dimensions of these stub pedals, making it all too easy to play two notes at a time. The pedal latch devices, like the M147, overcome this difficulty by giving priority to the lowest note played. Referring to the complete circuit (Fig. 3-76) the pedal oscillator IC applies 500 kHz to the pedal latch IC. This unit contains the logic required to generate five octave frequencies, (1, 2, 4, 8, 16) corresponding to the pedal pressed. Once a pedal is pressed, the audio output remains until a new pedal is used. In spite of the above, only the 2 and 4 ft. frequency outputs are actually used. The logic system operates as follows. Note there are 25 pedals, a full two octaves (musically very useful.) The octave change flip-flops change state each time an octave change occurs. Any pedal played in the C1 B1 range applies a low level to pin 13 of the IC. The output of this gate goes high and is applied to the low octave enable gate. This gate allows the 4 ft. signal

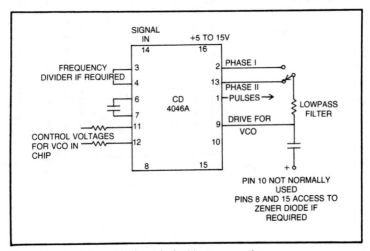

Fig. 3-75. The CD 4046A phase-locked loop connections.

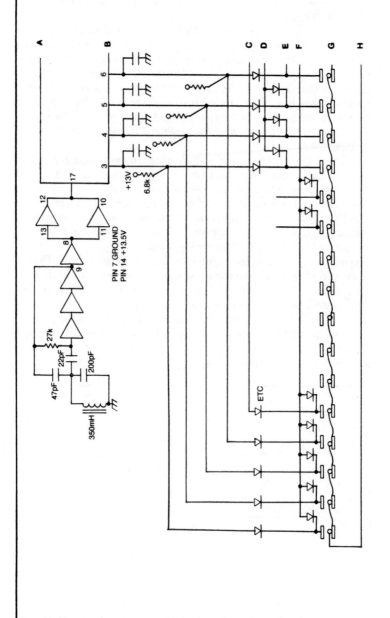

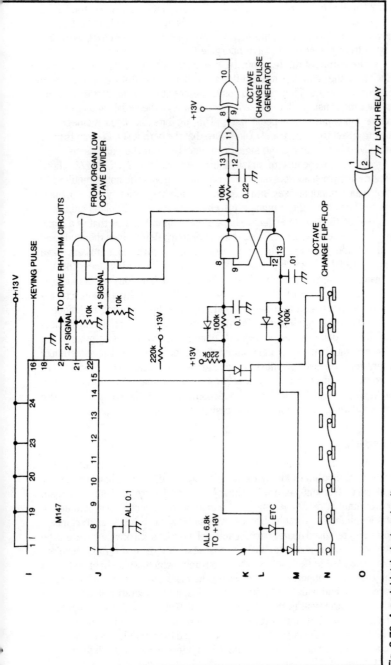

Fig. 3-76. A pedal latch device circuit.

87

pin 22 of the latch to pass to the pedal divider. Playing a pedal in the C2 C3 range causes the octave change flip-flop to change state and pin 10 if the IC now goes high applied to pin 2 of the octave enable gate this now lets the 2 ft signal from pin 21 of the latch energize the pedal divider.

The output of the IC at pin 10 is also applied to the input of the gate. Each time the octave change flip-flop alters state, pin 10 of the IC changes to high or low levels. This causes a positive pulse at its output for the duration of the time constant. This pulse is routed through the pedal switches to the active input pin of the pedal latch. This inhibits the latch momentarily during an octave change and makes sure that the output select circuits have stabilized before any audio signal can emerge from the pedal latch.

Other microchips of musical interest are the AY-5-1317A chord generator, which accepts one full octave and outputs the notes required to form major, minor and seventh chords. This unit has a priority system, the C major chord having the highest priority. The AY-1-1320 piano chip is of interest as the envelope decay shape closely approximates that of a piano and it is velocity sensitive, i.e., the *rate* of touch determines the loudness, and not the *pressure*. One or two organ and synthesizer makers have engineered their own chips, some of which are very complex indeed like the Wurlitzer, Chord, rhythm and keyer chips; but the functions are the same as have been explained in the foregoing text. It is merely a manufacturing convenience related to assembly and probably dip soldering techniques.

An interesting chip is the M251 of SGS-ATES; from this 40 pin unit it is possible to obtain arpeggios, chords of all kinds (automatic or otherwise,) bass accompaniments, trigger outputs for other apparatus, and selection of operating modes for playing keys, including memorization of selected keys to form chords automatically or to provide an automatic bass for any group of keys played. The ordering code number is M251 B1 ac for plastic encapsulation, or D1 for ceramic casing.

AMPLIFIERS

All electronic music generators require amplifiers. We are all familiar with large amplifiers for radio, record players, etc. The signals from any musical instrument pass through many channels before they enter the main power amplifiers. At one time it was common to connect as many circuits to one amplifier as possible, because valves or vacuum tubes were cumbersome and required heater current and high voltages, all of which were to be avoided as far as possible. With the advent of the transistor, rapid development soon led to the compact miniature units which are so light and small they can be supported in the wiring in many cases. One of the most successful, and widely used in all countries, is the operational amplifier of which the archtype is the 741. This circuit features high gain, high input resistance and low output resistance. There are balanced internal devices which discriminate against hum and noise, and the amplifier can be used for dc as well as ac amplification. These amplifiers have a very high inherent gain, possibly 100,000 times. This makes it possible to have very stable amplification by using an equally high amount of negative feedback (up to 100%.) If the bias conditions are properly set, then gain is then the ohmic value of the feedback resistor divided by the ohmic value of the input resistor. For almost all musical circuitry, the property of differential amplification does not arise, so that only one input is used. A balanced power supply is to be preferred. This allows the non-inverting or positive input to be at ground potential. The 741 and its derivatives are small signal amplifiers, the load should not exceed 10 mA and the power dissipation 400 mW. Fortunately the 741 is internally protected against short circuits, and this protection operates as long as the short remains.

The frequency range depends on the gain-bandwidth product and for the 741, this is about 1 MHz. So if the voltage gain was 1, one could obtain this bandwidth (that is, from 1 MHz down to dc). There would be a bandwidth of 100 kHz for a gain of 10, 10 kHz for a gain of 100, and so on. These figures apply only to small signals. All such chips have a slew rate depending on the physical properties of the materials of which the unit is made. Some redesign has resulted in the 748, which has a better performance, and there are similar chips by various makers. For music, the above are adequate. The slew rate is the value of the maximum rate of change of output voltage. Feedback does not affect this, so the bandwidth of the amplifier for large signals is less than for small signals. It is clear that the slew rate makes the 741 unsuitable for fast-rising pulses or square waves, but within the frequency bands used for music it is satisfactory. One could not use it with some digital circuitry, but the 748 and some other designs work well; e.g., type LS201.

It is not proposed to show any power or large amplifiers suitable for electronic music, there are many sources of data for those interested in building their own. Usually, large amplifiers are not voltage controlled, there is nothing very novel about them. Several of the devices shown so far have small signal amplifiers incorporated into them, but here is an example of a very useful low power amplifier using the 748 chip. It has a balanced input which improves the linearity and offsets any internal noise or hum pickup. The voltage control range would be from 0V to about 10V and it can accept several input signals at the same time. The power supply is single-sided. Figure 3-77 shows the circuit and its power requirements. The transistors can be 2N2222 or an IC, type 3054 dual pair.

Current designs of synthesizers are now so complicated that it is not thought good policy to reproduce any complete circuits here; one model is hardly on the market before it is superceded by a later one, so it is best to deal with the separate parts of these devices. The microprocessor is likely to prove a useful tool for music, at this time its use is mostly confined to melodic or one note at a time instruments, but it will develop; However some amusement can be derived from simpler circuits like the tune generator shown in Fig. 3-78. There are three parts; a pulse generator, a decade counter, and an audio frequency oscillator supplying a loudspeaker. The supply voltage is 9V, well decoupled. TR1 and TR2 form the pulse unit, the unijunction transistor acting as a relaxation oscillator, the frequency

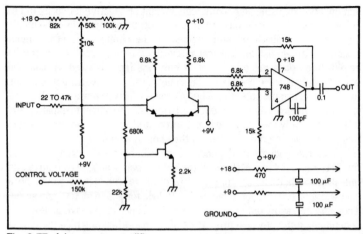

Fig. 3-77. A low power amplifier.

being selected from VR1 setting. TR2 amplifies this and acts as a switching transistor to advance the decade counter, consisting of IC1 and IC2. IC1 counts the pulses appearing at pin 14 and presents this in binary at pins 8, 9, 11, and 12. The 7490 counts from zero, and as shown, resets to 0 after 9 to make full use of IC2. This chip converts the binary output of IC1 to decimal in the ten output pins, each of which drops in turn to about the potential of the supply rail, the other nine remaining at a very high resistance.

Transistors TR3 and TR4 are an oscillator producing an audio frequency square wave which is amplified by TR3 to feed the loudspeaker. If now the time constant at the base of TR3 is changed, the frequency of oscillation will change as the decade counter goes through its cycle of

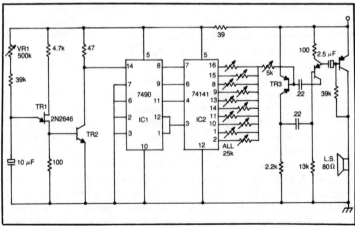

Fig. 3-78. A tune generator circuit.

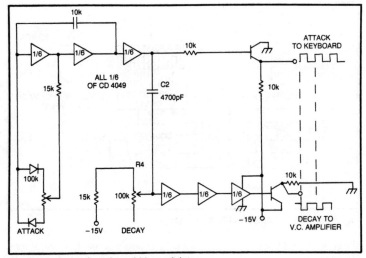

Fig. 3-79. A simple pulse-width modulator.

operations. This is done by connecting ten variable resistors in the outputs of IC2 and if these are set up for different notes, a tune can be programmed into the device. With the values shown, the note coverage is almost two octaves.

Pulse width modulation is an expression rather freely used; but in a simple form it can be used to control the attack and decay of all notes on the keyboard. The principle is that if one rapidly switches resistors in and out of the voltage-controlled amplifier channel, the apparent value of the resistors greatly increases. That is, if a 10k resistor is in circuit at all times, its effective value is 10k, but if it is in circuit only 10% of the time, its effective value is 100,000 ohms. In this circuit there is a hex inverter CD4049 and two drive transistors. The attack portion is a variable duty cycle oscillator operating at 400 Hz. The length of time that the attack remains grounded determines the attack time as a ratio of the total time. The leading edge of the attack waveform can be shortened by decay variable R4 and capacitor C2. The attack goes to the keyboard, while the decay goes to the voltage-controlled amplifier. The attack time has priority over the decay, so a key fully depressed charges the capacitor which is storing the attack and decay information. Quite a wide range of envelope control is possible with this simple circuit shown in Fig. 3-79.

A somewhat more refined pulse width modulator is illustrated in Fig. 3-80. It is digital in operation but analog in manipulation. The great advantage of this kind of circuit is that the envelope desired can be set up instantly and by making a card template, can always be repeated. The 16 counts of the 8288 counter are enabled by the input time reference of the start-stop oscillator. Each count is then decoded and sent to a slider type potentiometer. These pots can then be set to "draw" the waveform needed, the total

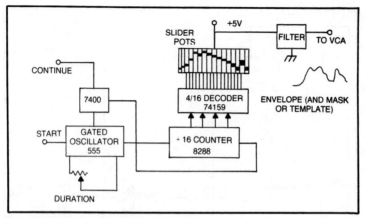

Fig. 3-80. A digital pulse-width modulator.

duration of the envelope being set by the frequency of the time references. When the key is released, the note will continue through the decay cycle. The advantage of this analog readout (the position of the knobs of the pots) is that one can produce any kind of envelope shape, perhaps quite unlike any known attack and decay times. Naturally, the more pots the more exact the envelope could be, but 16 give many variations. The physical shape of the curve of the knobs should be used to cut a template so that this curve can be repeated at will; it is rather like the curves of the old type Hammond organs, by which drawbars could be quickly set up to give all kinds of tonal variations.

If one has a number of similar small signal voltage-controlled amplifiers (as is very likely with several oscillators and filters in a simple synthesizer) then a convenient way of adding them together and including a master gain control, also voltage operated, is shown in Fig. 3-81. All the vca outputs can be shorted together as shown, but the input to the 3080 should not exceed 100 mV peak-to-peak when several notes are played simultaneously. This can be set by the value of R1. The possible range of control voltage may be from +15V (maximum gain) to −15V (off.) Of course, the signal at the summing resistors need not all be from oscillators, they could include noise, tremolo or other amplitude modulated effects.

Not all integrated circuits are small. LSI or *large scale integration* is certain to make progress for music, just as it has for computers. One example available now is the General Instrument Corporation's programmable sound generator, type AY-3-8910. It contains all the tone and noise generators, mixers, shift registers, interfacing connections for a microprocessor, envelope generators, digital to analog converters, decoding devices, and other elements, from which virtually any musical sound or noise can be produced at will. It is a foretaste of techniques to centralize and compact all the functions required of a synthesizer with means to effect control by means other than a keyboard; everything depends on what the

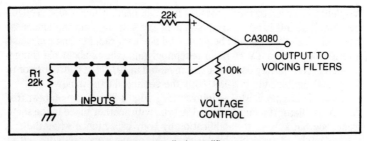

Fig. 3-81. Combining voltage-controlled amplifiers.

microprocessor is asked to do. As mentioned before, progress in this art is so rapid that even the above elaborate IC may soon become obsolescent, but it has great possibilities for today. However, in spite of its versatility, it is not polyphonic (that is, able to play more than one note at a time) and this limits its use for musical instruments. On the whole, the amateur is better served with separate chips for each required function.

So far, control of suitable circuitry has been envisaged as a matter of contacts and playing keys; though a simple circuit could be played on printed board "keys" or pads with a stylus. At one time there were many variations on the simple gold or alloy contact wire block, involving graphite resistors, impregnated felt, liquid resistances, etc. Now all is voltage-controlled, for even if keying is carried out by diodes or transistors, it is still dc keying. This chapter is concluded with a revival of the Theremin, a contactless music system devised nearly sixty years ago, but brought up to date with semiconductors. It must be understood that it is strictly a "fun" machine. It is surprising what a competent manipulator can do with it. The

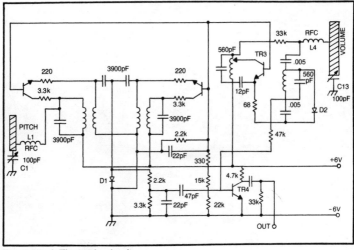

Fig. 3-82. A Theremin circuit.

frequency is varied by the position of the right hand, which is also used for tremolo. The left hand controls stopping and starting, and the loudness. Note that the circuit should be in a metal box as it radiates and can cause interference with a TV or radio reception. And talking about old things, recall that the Hartley oscillator was invented in 1917, the multivibrator in 1918, and the bistable in 1919. Only the semiconductor is new!

The Theremin works as follows (See Fig. 3-82.) It uses a beat frequency oscillator running at about 150 kHz, with another tuned to the same frequency but subject to modification by body capacitance when the rod marked pitch is approached by the hand. This detunes one oscillator and an audio note is formed in the well-known way by the difference frequency. TR4 is a small signal amplifier which now accepts this signal. When the other hand is brought near the rod marked volume, the oscillator of TR3 is retuned and as the impedance of L4 and C13 increases, the rf voltage from TR3 also increases. This voltage is rectified by D2 and applied to the base of TR4 as a control bias (the gain varies as the voltage varies.) The waveform is very rich in harmonics and although the instrument is very difficult to play, many fascinating and strange effects are possible which cannot be obtained in any other way.

Chapter 4

Electronic Music and the Composer

It must not be thought that the desire for greater flexibility in the limitations of the musical scale is of recent origin. Musicians for years have been dissatisfied with tonal limitations and we find Busoni and Schönberg, for instance, conceiving the ideas of an infinite tonal spectrum and an infinite tone color relationship regardless of the method to fulfill it. Of course this is impossible with conventional orchestral instruments. Busoni himself said that "further development is impossible with our present instruments." Nevertheless, Anton Webern did pursue the idea further, merging it with his concept of the proportional series in which both the harmonic and the melodic employ the same interval proportional series so that the consonances no longer depend on arbitrary or statistical factors but on harmonic ratios, i.e., on acoustical structures which conform to the law of the permutation of series, series being defined as an ordered set of parameter values; and serial structures being formed by varying two or more parameters in discrete steps, giving to each of the parameters values taken in order from the series chosen for the parameter in question. The structure is called complete when it contains all possible combinations of parameter values.

Many of Webern's constructions seem like premature electronic fragments. His permutations of sounds lead directly to the question of shaping sounds by the grouping of sinusoidal tones. A sinusoidal tone is in a way, a misnomer; such sounds are pure sine waves and as such, have no "tone." They are the basis of all musical sound processes, but as such are no more than an imagined system of reference from which the composer builds structures in the form of sequences, ratios, series and classes.

But electronic music is not twelve tone music, it embraces an infinitely greater number of combinational possibilities. Accordingly, it is even more atonal than atonal music, but does not share its shock effects. While creating relationships between the elements, it appears atonal or abstract when judged by the standards of traditional harmonies, which again means that the infinite number of tonal subdivisions possible fall strangely on ears attuned to the semitone scale—or even the tenth tone scale. The fact that these seemingly abstract forms are derived from a naturalistic all-tone sound material, constitutes the unique property of electronic music. If indeed the elements of music are a shapeless plastic mass, as suggested by Helmholtz in the preface, then electronic music facilities can join the elemental to the ordered side of sound by reaching into chaos and drawing forth the very foundation plans of music.

The complex tone with harmonic partials is composed of a succession of harmonic partials, each of which is in itself a sinusoid. The "tone" of an instrument is not a tone at all, but a sound which is determined by the frequency components which contribute to the timbre. By electronic means, we can, for the first time, make these components variable.

In the simple tone mixture the frequencies of the partials are not harmonically related to the fundamentals; they cannot be expressed in terms of integral ratios. However, mixtures are still mixtures of sinusoidal tones and hence are not to be confused with chords. They can be turned into musical sound much more readily than instrumental chords. Conventional instrumental musical tone mixtures do not persist—they start, maintain for a time, then decay. By electronic means, steady tone mixtures are easily possible.

NOISE

Noise has character and to some extent, pitch. "Colored" noise has musically positional relationship; but white noise, extending over the entire range of audibility has no pitch position. Colored noise, that is, noise with a tone superimposed (or the reverse) has many uses in composition.

Two different sounds given simultaneously produce an interval, more than two, a chord. In conventional music complex tone and interval are clearly distinguishable from one another. In electronic music, however, the tone mixture with its high "binding" level forms a bridge between the two. Sounds and mixtures can be composed electronically, not according to the standard of the natural scheme of things or according to the theories of harmony, but according to a prescribed composition arrangement. But, to compose successfully, a good deal of knowledge of a kind not usually found among musicians may be required. This includes familiarity with the operation of the equipment and some knowledge of electro-acoustics, which is quite different from the case where a composer makes himself familiar with the technique of the violin or trumpet, with a view to composing for these instruments. Whether he regards any kind of apparatus as his "instrument" now, or whether he considers tape recording as the new technical form of composing, the fact that he is no longer moving in a solidly constructed tonal system places him in a quite new situation. He finds himself able to shape the musical material in his mind to embrace all known and unknown, possible and imaginable sounds; and this of course makes it necessary to think in these new dimensions. Tradition may now be discarded; it is for the musician alone now to decide whether the acoustic material which will evolve from his electronic manipulations shall contain those elements of order which in the traditional sense can be called elements of music. But the basic building blocks can be re-oriented pitchwise to maintain all the timbres with their rich variations, and at the same time to give tremendous dynamic range, tempi and brilliance of figures not subject to human limitations, complete freedom to use and combine any rhythms or accents, unlimited percussions, noise and quasi-musical waveforms, the use, for the first time in music, of the pure sinusoid as a "tone" on its own, and all the other subjective attributes of music.

Clearly what has been said relates to man-made music. It is possible to compose by a machine, and much work has been done on this aspect. But a machine cannot think, and composition is a mental process. If sufficient information is fed to the right kind of machine, an order of probability results which could be interpreted as a form for deriving musical sounds. This indeed has been done, but if the information follows a known pattern then the machine must produce a similar pattern even if it is different in some ways. A machine is well suited to providing a formal structure underlying the composition, indeed it can do little else. This must be considered a limitation, since above all else, electronic systems are completely devoid of form. Therefore a composer must bear in mind that the main basic parameters are frequency, intensity and time. All else derives from these.

As has been said, composing is a mental process and therefore personal and not possible of communication to another except in the form of a realization of that process in sound. It is not possible to lay down any rules of composition, but this must be regarded as a situation which opens up an unparalleled vista of possibilities because of the flexibility of the medium. Suppose one were told that any sound of any kind, within the limits of audibility, could be constructed, and that any number of such sounds could be added, together or serially, in any way for any length of time and with any kind of loudness level or range, would not this tend to inspire a composer to forget convention and to seek means to fulfill his hitherto limited ambitions? Even the most conservative musician can at once point to many orchestral limitations which he would like to see removed. Consider, too, the convenience. Instead of having to write many copies of a score, and obtain the services of the required number of musicians, the composer can do all this himself at the cost only of time and inexpensive materials. Further, he can modify and rewrite any part of his work until perhaps a number of interpretations have been prepared, from which he can select. It is not even possible to detail the incredible flexibility of this art.

The facilities available to the composer will determine how far he can go, but systems which store the composition before committing it to tape are to be preferred, since at any instant the previously constructed sounds can again be played and altered prior to permanent recording.

RCA SOUND SYNTHESIZER

With the RCA sound synthesizer (Figs. 4-1 and 4-2,) there is a permanent record on paper, which at the same time is the master producing the effects. Although a musician with little or no knowledge of electronics can operate this device, it is very desirable to know what the use of the various controls actually does from an electrical aspect; this is analogous to a composer writing for strings without having studied the range of notes possible and the effect of various kinds of bowing, vibrato, etc.

The initial control of the synthesizer resides in the programming input device, where the properties of the components necessary—frequency, envelope, spectrum, intensity, duration, etc.—are specified in the form of binary code instructions, holes punched in a fifteen-inch wide paper roll by keys mounted on a keyboard and arranged in ten vertical columns of four keys each. On the apparatus shown in Fig. 4-1 there are two complete keyboards, so that two programs can be simultaneously recorded. The first column of keys represents sixteen binary choices and controls frequency, that is, one element of a frequency class. The second column selects "octave," that is, the position in the tonal spectrum of the frequency chosen. The third column selects envelope, which is the growth, steady-state (if any) and decay characteristics to any desired extent. The fourth column selects the spectrum, or actual tone quality, and the last column selects the intensity.

Those who recall the perforated paper rolls used for the player-piano or pianola will remember that sustained notes were obtained by an elon-

Fig. 4-1. RCA Electronic Music Synthesizer Mark II located at Columbia-Princeton Electronic Music Center.

Fig. 4-2. RCA perforator.

gated slot. The action being pneumatic, this allowed holding up of the striking mechanism or dampers, but with all electric system where great accuracy is required, slots allow the paper to deform and perhaps tear. Accordingly, an ingenious system of wire brushes above each hole is so arranged that, if a series of holes follows along the same vertical line in close proximity, the contacts made by the brushes do not open until after the last hole is passed. Thus one can sustain a parameter as long as required without slotting the roll.

Pressure on the keys allotted to each section of the roll punches a hole through which the brushes and relays control the output of the frequency generators. There are twelve of these consisting of electrically driven tuning forks tuned to the equal temperament frequencies from 2903 to 3591 Hz. These fixed oscillators are available for any composer who wishes to use equal temperament. There are also twenty-four variable frequency oscillators, tunable from 8130 to 16180 Hz. Any required division of the octave is possible from these circuits, and any octave is possible from the "octaver" section of the roll by suitable punching.

The fixed oscillators have multipliers to raise the useful frequency range. There is also a white noise generator to provide random noise. After passing through the "octavers" the waveform is converted to a sawtooth, which means that each original frequency now contains a complete spectrum of harmonic partials (non-tempered,) in phase, and with the amplitude of each partial related inversely to its numerical position in the spectrum. It is from this sawtooth that the filters of the spectrum section of the roll finalize the tone color called for.

Passing to the third column of the roll, we have the envelope control. This consists of a series of resistance-capacity networks, whose time constants determine the rate of change of growth (or attack) and decay. Growth times are from 1 millisecond to 2 seconds, and decay times are from 4 milliseconds to 19 seconds. There is an infinite variety of times possible so that the slope of a sound can be made to conform to any law—not necessarily to any law of nature. For example, one could have a sound starting very rapidly, then, before settling down to any steady rate, it could be made to slow down or alter its "loudless" curve in any way at all. Thus a multitude of quite new effects is possible, even from one single tone or frequency, just by altering the envelope. This is just one of the points where the synthesizer scores heavily over conventional instruments, for it would be impossible to change the initiation of the sound on, say, an oboe.

Passing now to the next column of keys, there is the spectrum or timbre section. Here we encounter the vibrato or tremolo unit, high and low pass filters, and the main formant or resonating circuits which can be set up by means of patch cords to give 9^{10} different resonance conditions; there are also attenuators here, patchable to give 6^{10} different attenuation positions. Recalling that the synthesizers provide eight such panels, there are 8 times 15^{10} possible filter settings—surely enough to perform any forseeable operation on a sawtooth waveform! But, added to this, is the facility for adding in noise and the introduction of the vibrato. It can be argued that the value of the tremolo is not so great as coding contrasting intensity values on the keyboard; but when three or four tremolo units, each with differing frequency values are cascaded or combined in rerecording, then the complex periodic result is extremely difficult to approximate by intensity coding and of course different tremolo rates can be applied to different frequency components of a single spectrum, through the many filters.

Once a spectrum has been shaped, the resulting signal is taken to one of sixteen amplifier channels. Here again, there is infinite latitude in relating the loudness of one component to another, although this would normally be fixed by the intensity code punchings.

To code his composition, then, the composer first assigns values to the code number for each component, certainly to the ones he intends to use right away. To do this, switches are provided above the keyboard, in rows of four each parameter. They act on the same relays as the brushes. Thus, the aural effect of the sound set up can be tested before actually committing it to the roll. When he is satisfied, he then punches the roll, and plays it back by hand, cranking it across the brushes. It will be recalled that the brushes only operate relays, so that the speed at which the roll is moved cannot influence the pitch, unlike altering the speed of a tape or disc; therefore the effect can be carefully analyzed, and correction is possible to a limited extent. For example, holes not wanted can be stopped off with masking tape, and there may be room to punch further parameter holes if some of the values are not correct. By these means, a sound spectrum or composition can be built up note by note until the composer is satisfied. The motor can then be started and the roll played at the normal speed of four inches per second; the duration of a roll is about five minutes. Of course, this represents a straightforward composition process, but the playback speed may be varied, and the roll could even be run backwards. Disc recording was originally provided, but it has been found more convenient to use a synchronized tape multi-track machine. If, for example, two keyboards were in use at the same time, then at least seven tracks could be independently recorded on this machine. Then, the outputs could be combined and rerecorded another seven times. This now produces 49 series of tones. One more step would give 343 series, which is a very complex tone band. There is, in fact, no limit to the synthesis possibilities of the RCA instrument. An example of tonal synthesis, not possible with physical instruments, might be if we took binary 1 to be C, binary 2 = C plus a quarter of a tempered whole tone, binary 3 = C plus one eighth of a tempered whole tone, and binary 4 be C plus a tempered whole tone (that is, D.) Then, by transposing circuit number 1, these tones would not be transposed in the same ratio but by some permutation of the original pitch class.

We have not so far mentioned the gliding or portamento circuits, which enable continuous transition from one frequency to another, as for example in the trombone. This circuit can be patched in to modify any punched steady tone although this requires that more than one person manipulate the controls. Thus we can see that it is easily possible for a composer to "try out" a new work with quite arbitrary tone colors just to get his succession of notes and harmonics correct, all before making a permanent punched record. The appearance of such a roll is seen in Fig. 4-3, which shows a phrase of a composition for electronic music and carries the punching instructions to clarify the procedure. In this example, alternate notes are given to left and right channels of the machine. Equivalence with conventional notation is also shown in the drawing. Given a paper speed of four inches per second, sixteen holes per second can pass under the brushes. The normal length for a quarter note is then four holes on one inch in order to play at a metronome speed of 240 quarter notes to the minute. One must be careful to note these speeds, for the tape recorder is synchronously driven by the apparatus, and while there can be no alteration in pitch if the keyboard slows down or speeds up, it would be disastrous if the tape speed varied when later the composition was played back on a standard machine. We might add that to ensure synchronization, the tape has sprocket holes for the master recording.

Although the perforated roll is quick and easy for an unskilled operator, certain advantages accrue from continuous marking as in the figure appended, where lines are drawn in reflecting ink, to determine the limits of the parameters to be controlled (Fig. 4-4.) Small exciter lamps and photocells mounted above removed the information and cause relays to operate the respective parameter racks.

We have seen that the RCA machine is a storage device, and another example is the Oramic graphic system. Whereas with RCA all the parameters are combined on one master perforated control element, in Miss Oram's

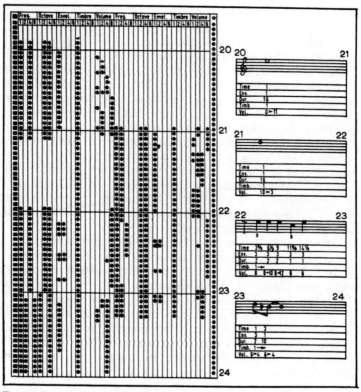

Fig. 4-3. Punched information for RCA Music Synthesizer. Setting-up procedure described on right.

device all the parameters are individually compiled although mechanically coupled; therefore any one (or more than one) parameter can be removed from the realization at any time and, like RCA, all can be stored after final processing of the sound event.

ORAMIC SYSTEM

The idea is very simple; basically there is a series of transparent perforated film strips, all spaced out above a table or platform and all passing over sprockets attached to a common feed and a common takeup shaft. By means of opaque adhesive tape, or by drawing with a felt pen if desired, information is imparted to such strips as may be required. On rotating the shafts, all tracks move together from right to left and pass over photocells which are constantly illuminated. The patterns on the various tracks then modulate the steady light and give rise to corresponding voltage or current changes in the photocell outputs. These changes now control devices which are the basic parameters; oscillators, envelope shapers, intensity and so on. Timbre or waveform is controlled in an ingenious manner. The oscillator waveforms are supplied to cathode ray tubes, the pattern appearing on the screens. A glass plate, carrying an opaque mask of the desired type, is placed over the tube face. The outline of the scanned waveform on the mask is seen by a photomultiplier, which superimposes this signal on the frequency outlets of however many oscillators are being used as pitch sources, for there are several cathode ray scanners. A mask can be instantly removed and changed and herein lies the extreme versatility, because *any* waveshape can be drawn or otherwise applied to the glass plates.

Now since all the functions emanating from the photocells are merely control currents, it does not matter at what rate the tracks are moving—except that analog tracks such as duration, vibrato and envelope control will have different values. Digital tracks such as timbre, frequency and intensity will not be affected. Therefore having graphically processed one or more tracks, the whole series can be moved across the photocells quite slowly, by a handwheel, to evaluate the resulting sound. Any modification is easily

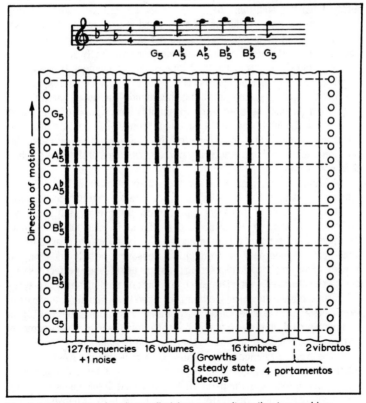

Fig. 4-4. Ink marking for photocell pickup as an alternative to punching.

and quickly carried out by stripping off the tape and applying more in any required manner. Note that the tape does not require great accuracy in cutting. The frequency control, for example, must be correctly placed vertically, i.e., as if it were a note written on a conventional music sheet. But the actual size and shape are not important; the envelope shaping track controls the onset of the sound, the intensity track governs the loudness.

Two features of this system which are probably more sensitive and accurate than in any other synthesizer or composing machine are the envelope and vibrato tracks. Because the gradients or rates of change can conform to any contour of the opaque part of the track, very fine nuances are possible. This overcomes the somewhat "mechanical" nature of certain electronically composed music.

To revert to the apparatus proper. The track sprockets for either feed or takeoff are secured to spindles running in accurate bearings. Those on the right draw unused film from the magazines up to the graphic table. Normally there would be three frequency tracks, one envelope shaping track, one intensity track and one vibrato track. Further source controls, e.g., noise coloration or adjustable filters, would require further tracks, a' perfectly feasible addition. The frequency tracks each carry several notes arranged in the same order as on a standard music stave. The relative spacing between them must be worked out in association with the usual track speed of 10 cm/sec, which is obtained in a perfectly steady manner from a motor driving through a clutch for easy disengagement. However, no sound could in any case be heard until the duration track operates, for this controls the gating system initiating the sound—the attack circuit. The expression "sound" is used here to simplify description of the signal parameters, though of course the resultant "sound" is a mixture of all the tracks and is not audible until required. It is because of the action of the duration track gate that the accuracy of the front edges of the note patches need not be too great.

A schematic diagram of the synthesis path is shown in Fig. 4-5 from which it is apparent that the individual tracks are separately recorded as in Fig. 4-6. This might at first sight appear to call for a very costly recorder, but in fact by striping the same kind of film as is used for the graphic information and running this over another set of sprockets geared to the same shafts, synchronous recording must ensue. It is only necessary to provide recording heads and a spring pressure plate, when perfectly satisfactory results can be obtained. Since playback or reading heads are available after the recording heads, either the mixed track signals or any part of them can be heard at once. Clearly any or all of this information could again be mixed into the amplifier input or to ring modulators to give very complex patterns, and of course artificial reverberation is available.

One great advantage of the Oramic system is that the mechanics are relatively simple, being a good engineering project for a university or similar institution, as all the parts can be purchased. If one takes recording facilities into account, this system is probably the least expensive of any,

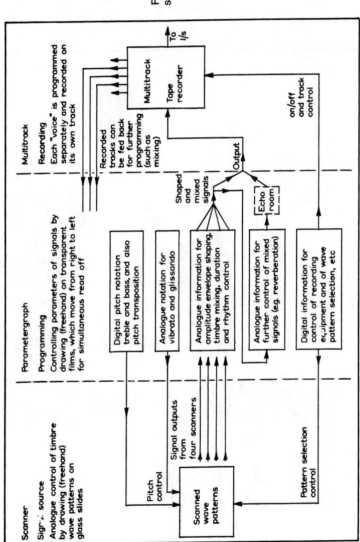

Fig. 4-5. Oramics graphic sound.

Scanner

Signal source

Analogue control of timbre by drawing (freehand) wave patterns on glass slides

Parametergraph

Programming

Controlling parameters of signals by drawing (freehand) on transparent films, which move from right to left for simultaneous read off

Multitrack

Recording

Each "voice" is programmed separately and recorded on its own track

Recorded tracks can be fed back for further programming (such as mixing)

To l/s

Multitrack

Tape recorder

on/off and track control

Shaped and mixed signals

Output

Digital pitch notation treble and bass, and also pitch transposition

Analogue notation for vibrato and glissando

Analogue information for amplitude envelope shaping, timbre mixing, duration and rhythm control

Analogue information for further control of mixed signals (eg. reverberation)

Echo room

Digital information for control of recording equipment and of wave pattern selection, etc

Pitch control

Signal outputs from four scanners

Scanned wave patterns

Pattern selection control

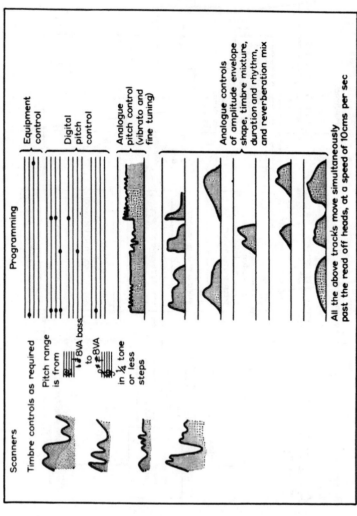

Fig. 4-6. Expansion of Fig. 4-5.

though of course it is not portable. The teaching facilities are extremely good, especially for harmony and counterpoint, because perfectly conventional methods of composition can be displayed as well as the limitless parameters of electronic music, and with this system any one part of the tonal spectrum can be removed or altered without affecting the remainder. The apparatus is protected by worldwide patents.

Figure 4-7 is a photograph of the writing and transport parts of the mechanism, and the reading photocells are to the left inside the light-tight black box, with their photomultipliers beneath. Note signal tracks nearest to the bottle of ink, with control tracks on the upper four strips of film.

It would be reasonable to recommend the Oramic system for one without long experience in this artform, because here the information is in the form of adhesive opaque tape and so is easily removed and repositioned. Moreover, what has been synthesized can be immediately played back by hand at any speed, even a crawling speed, to judge the effect. The speed of replay has no effect on the pitch, though clearly the actual speed will affect the senses and so apportion values to the sound. The reader will recall that transparent 35 mm cine film is the basic medium for this device, so that the advantage of sprocket holes can be realized. For any multiple track system, it is essential to have perfect synchronization between tracks, and this is best attainable by perforated material.

The composer must bear in mind that the transfer of the limits of musical composition from the existing lines of the nonelectric medium and the human performer to this most extensive and flexible of media imposes its own limits in the form of far less well-understood limits—the perceptual and conceptual capacities of the human auditor. An electronic composition pushed to the limits of the apparatus may cause frustration and bewilderment on account of the radical departure from traditional laws and the production of stimuli to which the auditory system is not accustomed, the most difficult parameter to assimilate being the infinite gradations of the

Fig. 4-7. Writing and transport parts of Oramic Graphic System.

time scale possible, upsetting all concepts of rhythm and tempo (in a traditional sense.) This is because of the property of electronic systems to hold a note indefinitely, or to make it so short of duration that it is hardly audible. The composer must get used to the interval controlling and envelope system of the machine he is using.

SERIAL SOUND STRUCTURE GENERATOR

Let us look at the requirements for a serial sound structure generator. A serial sound structure generator (SSSG) is an electronic system designed to apply serial logic to parameters which characterize musical sounds so that the composer may evaluate the result. It does not produce complete compositions, but in what follows the composer can hear the sound structure at once and modify any part of it at will. We have already explained the meaning of parameter, series, serial structure etc. The maximum variations structure is a complete structure in which no two adjacent parameter values are the same. Such a structure can only exist when for any two series A and B in the group of series, the number of terms in A and the number of terms in B have no common factor. If for example three series have 10, 11 and 12 terms, there is a common factor of 2 between the first and last. This could not be a continuous structure. In Table 4-1, let four parameters A, B, C, and D be the variables. The numbers in the center column could be used to describe the sound event and would mean that the A parameter had the value shown by the fourth term in the A series, the B terms had the value given by the first term in the B series, and so on. If the parameters shown on the right side of the block were used, the sound event would have a duration as shown by the fourth term in the duration series, and so on. The simple example of a serial sound structure complete is shown in Fig. 4-8. Here there are two series, the duration series having two terms only; term J is a half note duration, term 2 a quarter note duration. The pitch series here has three terms: E4, G4, and C5. The complete structure contains six sound events, because the two series can be associated in six ways. So also it is clear that this is a maximum variation series, because there is no common factor to the number of terms in the two series. The notation used in Fig. 4-8 as well as the conventional musical notation is shown.

To execute the above, an electronic switching system is required, as in Fig. 4-9. Impulses are transmitted serially between the parameter switch banks, which have been previously set up to give the independent values of the example. At the end of the process, all is repeated again unless arrested

Parameter A	4	Duration
Parameter B	1	Pitch
Parameter C	3	Intensity
Parameter D	7	Timbre

Table 4-1. Notation for One Sound Event in a Serial Structure.

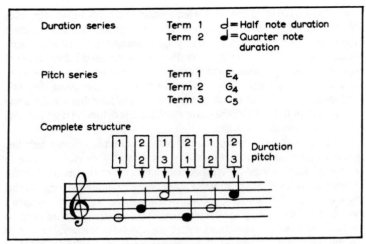

Fig. 4-8. A serial structure formed from two short series.

by some means. More complex series structures can of course be set up and explored in the same way, and hybrid structures are also possible, wherein some parameters are controlled by series while the remainder are controlled by other means, perhaps manually or by a random system. Of course, the pitch or frequency term in these experiments need not be a single tone, there might be frequency dividers to add octaves or there might be some other interval to the harmonics added, thus a complex chord could be formed for one pitch parameter.

Departing from the question of the mathematics of composition for a moment, consider music as a form of communication. Indeed this must be so, and in this case we can introduce the concept of entropy. Entropy is

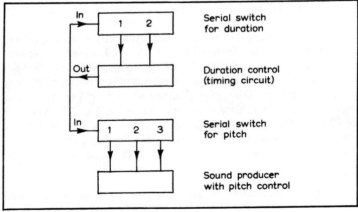

Fig. 4-9. Connection for structure in Fig. 4-8.

really the degree of randomness in any system. Where there is a high order of uncertainty, the entropy is high; where there is much similarity or even symmetry, the entropy is low. Melody must then be associated with a state of entropy sufficiently low that a definite pattern is established, yet high enough to have sufficient complexity to provide sophistication. In general, real music has a relatively low value of entropy and that being the case, statistical analysis can be carried out on simple melodies by the same composer; for if these melodies have stood the test of time, and are popular, then such an analysis is valid.

As an example of this approach, a number of Stephen Foster melodies were analyzed to ascertain the degree of entropy*. One might deduce in advance that there would be considerable similarity, and indeed a first order of approximation shows that twelve notes only are required to compose this type of melody. The frequency of occurrence of these twelve notes is shown in Fig. 4-10 which also gives the twelve notes in question. This information is based on eleven compositions, but all transposed to one key, D major, to ensure uniformity. However, if successive notes are chosen so that their probability depends on the preceding note, the structural becomes more complicated. But this is a more useful source of randomness data; see Table 4-2. In this example, the base of the probability was made sixteen because the analyzing machine had sixteen channels; otherwise there is no reason for the figure, but it does give a good spread to the values. For instance, the probability of B3 following D4 is so high that it is virtually a certainty. From this table, the style of the composer is evident. The analysis can be extended to the probability of three note sequences. It could be further extended, but taking the three note sequence referred to, and assuming there are trinotes ABA, ABB and ABC occurring 7, 14 and 13 times respectively, this makes a total of 34. Thus, there are 7 chances in 34 that A will follow AB; or 3 chances in 16 (expressed in sixteenths) that A will follow AB.

Rhythm can also be analyzed in a similar manner because rhythm is a series of impulses repeated to some pattern; therefore an order of probability results—that is, where there is any defined pattern.

It is then possible to design a composing machine based on a random selection of notes determined by a probability based on preceding events. Without going into such a device in detail, it can be pointed out that the basic instrument is a random number generator, which is useful for all forms of musical composition. One way of doing this is to connect four free-running multivibrators to four bistable multivibrators as in Fig. 4-11. MVI to 4 oscillate continuously, and as they feed the bistables B1 to 4, should a multivibrator be disconnected from its bistable, the transistors of this latter unit would remain conductive in one branch of the circuit. If some form of

---

*Figures 4-10, 4-11, 4-12, Table 4-2 and some of the text relating to the Stephen Foster analysis are from *Music, Physics and Engineering*, by H. F. Olson, and reproduced by permission of Dover Publications, New York.

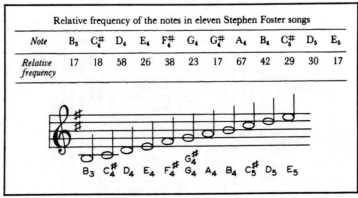

Note	B₃	C#₄	D₄	E₄	F#₄	G₄	G#₄	A₄	B₄	C#₅	D₅	E₅
Relative frequency	17	18	58	26	38	23	17	67	42	29	30	17

Relative frequency of the notes in eleven Stephen Foster songs

Fig. 4-10. The notes of the musical scale used in the analysis of Stephen Foster songs.

switch connects and disconnects the various multivibrators from their bistables a few times a second, even if this is regularly recurring, the selection of frequencies from the bistables will be random because of the high frequency of the oscillation of the multivibrators compared with the frequency of operation of the switch or controller. Further, as one transistor of the bistable concerned is still conducting on opening the coupling from the drive, there is a standing current available which can be used for operating relays etc. It is clear that if the switch is connected to a random rhythm pattern generator, all forms of probability can be explored. There is no limit to the frequency range of the apparatus, multivibrators are easily tuned and the bistables should be aperiodic and thus will follow any change in injected frequency without adjustment. Of course, a decoding and memory machine could be added as a form of initial control and if this was so, then over a long period of time a definite pattern would result, depending on

Table 4-2. Two-Note Sequences of Eleven Stephen Foster Songs. Probability of Following Note*.

Note	B₃	C#₄	D₄	E₄	F#₄	G₄	G#₄	A₄	B₄	C#₅	D₅	E₅
B₃			16									
C#₄			16									
D₄	1	1	2	5	3	1		1		1	1	
E₄		1	6	3	4			1			1	
F#₄			2	4	5	2		2	1			
G₄					4	3		6	3			
G#₄								16				
A₄			1		5	1	1	4	3		1	
B₄			1		1	1		9	2		2	
C#₅									8		8	
D₅								4	7	3	1	1
E₅								6		10		

*Probability of not following the preceding note expressed in sixteenths.

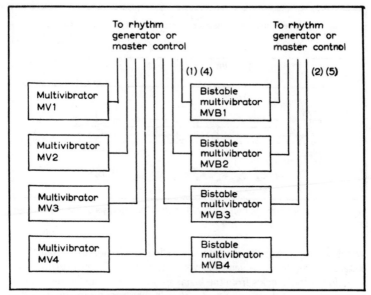

Fig. 4-11. Random number generator.

the information fed to the system, and this would repeat again and again until stopped. Usually the processed signals would be recorded on tape, and this again could be fed in as a control. There is no limit to the combinational powers of a system of this nature, save that there must be restrictions or screening of a mathematical nature applied to the random probability process otherwise the result would be nothing but random and quite meaningless. For instance, even if any musical substance resulted from the electronic operations, the value of the sound could be nil if it had no rhythm or tempo. There are 16 possible quarter-note rhythms in a common time measure alone, coding patterns for this time being shown in Fig. 4-12. These of course are very simple examples.

All of the foregoing methods require that the operator actually manipulates the independent facets of the information, perhaps painstakingly so far as complete assembly is concerned. These means are called tape music, there is nothing against it except that is very time-consuming. For a complex and complete work, it might mean months of assembly and much cutting and editing of tape. When the art was practiced on a very small scale and by few individuals, this was a valid approach.

The art of composing electronic music is tending towards methods which can specify the elements for the sound structure with the precision and range of the present-day synthesizers. In the forefront of such equipment is the computer, either of an all-digital type or having analog functions added. This latter must of course be part of the system to introduce the time factor on which the value of the fed-in information in terms of sound depends. Therefore samples of the sound wave to be heard are computed in the form of many numbers which are read out of the computer at a high speed (30,000 numbers per second to make a sound with a bandwidth of 15 kHz), and supplied to a digital to analog converter. The output pulses from the converter are smoothed by means of filters and can be heard from a loudspeaker via a suitable amplifying system. It is clear that this process is an extension of the simple analysis given previously. The principles are shown in Fig. 4-13. Of course, the system of providing, say, 30,000 numbers per second would (as such) be too tedious and does not necessarily give the control over the basic parameters which are acceptable. Therefore it is more convenient to program the synthesis by macro structures called "instruments." These could each be constructed from groups of oscillators,

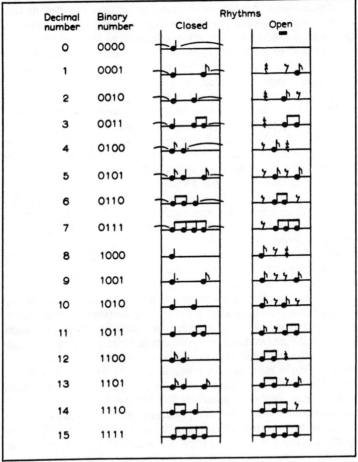

Fig. 4-12. Basic rhythmic scheme for 4/8 meter. (After Hiller and Isaacson).

noise generators, etc., and are used as unit instructions. Each unit is controlled by input numbers, being thus the equivalent of the voltage-controlled oscillators and other devices in analog synthesizers. Being in digital form, there is no restriction on performance speed, but at the same time, without a digital to analog converter system, there are no nuances or real time adjustment of the sound—it is supplied unalterable from the computer. The hybrid synthesizer solves these problems.

COMPUTERS AND MUSIC

A digital computer is provided with real time inputs which can be played by the musician-performer. A group of digital to analog converters provide a number of control signals for an analog synthesizer. Sound from the synthesizer is heard directly by the performer so that he can adjust sound qualities and introduce the amount of performance variation which he wishes. The control signals to the analog synthesizer are of sufficiently low bandwidth to make a much lower sampling rate from the converter necessary and thus the speed of the computer can be lower; the cost of such a computer can be less than that for all-digital synthesis. An alternative approach is possible to save computer time.

It will be understood that if the composing system is, let us say, in a university, then a number of music students may well be waiting to use it. Further, it is not improbable that original ideas may be lost if contained only in the head, should the waiting time be excessive. At best there must be frustration. Therefore instead of asking the computer to set up the whole of the waveforms, it can be made to generate voltages which control the instantaneous values of various parameters of the sound waveform, the actual waves themselves being generated by external apparatus. This method only requires a low bandwidth between the computer and the auxiliary equipment, and this allows real time operation with a quite small computer. Since however the control voltages are an indirect form of parameter control, drift and departure from exact frequency etc. might occur in the external equipment; therefore occasional checking and possibly recalibration is required.

The system comprises a computer and a digital to analog converter. The converter consists of a number of digital potentiometers which can be set in discrete steps, and which control oscillators by voltage increments. However, the pots are linear so an exponential converter changes the slope of the control voltage to approximate more to the logarithmic response of the ear. On the other hand, the gain controls of the voltage controlled amplifiers can be altered linearly or exponentially as required. Since there is a separate amplifier for each of the four oscillators simultaneously controlled, there is no risk of intermodulation. As is customary in methods involving direct current control, a push-pull or balanced amplifier is required to ensure there is no trace of the control signal in the output. Because the control originates in stepped potentiometers, there is a jump (however small) between increments of control voltage; this must be

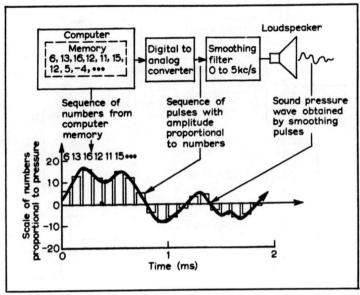

Fig. 4-13. Principle of computer composition. Scale on left is equivalent to loudness.

removed before it causes a jump in frequency, so following the pots are low pass filters which act as smoothing devices. There is a fixed time constant for these filters, so that the four processed signals will be in synchronism. It is 20 milliseconds, a good compromise between apparently instantaneous sound and the removal of transients. The computer timing can also be provided by a 40 Hz generator. The arrangement of this apparatus is as in Fig. 4-14.

Although there is a great simplification of the information supplied to this computer the same basic parameters must always be called up because all music processing depends on the essentials outlined many times: pitch or frequency, duration or envelope, intensity or loudness; and timbre and vibrato as second order ingredients. The combination of some or all of these basic parameters into "instruments" can be used to simplify the language for the computer, so that a wide range of possible characteristics can be controlled from a few input codes. Of course, as in all other systems, an over-riding manual facility is provided although modifications can be made by computer-operated switches if the information is correctly supplied. There is a manual mixer for the processed tones, which results in real time control.

As already mentioned, calibration and checking of the voltage-operated external sources may be required from time to time; the more voices combined at one time, the greater the need for accuracy. The computer can carry out instructions to ensure correct setting of the voltage

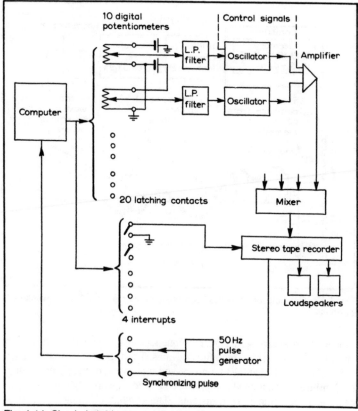

Fig. 4-14. Simple hybrid composing system.

pots, if suitably programmed. So, from the foregoing it can be seen that for very precise specification of waveform etc., a digital sampling technique is the best method; but using this kind of hybrid technique, sound compositions, especially those of an instrumental nature, can be accurately and economically programmed. Clearly the cost is reduced and certainly the saving in time (at the actual instrument) is very real. As with any punched information system, the preparatory setting up time away from the machine may be considerable, and this does not prevent the computer from being used by those already prepared.

Now if the composer is a conventional musician trained in the conventional methods of writing and scoring, then if he is going to pursue electronic composition, it is almost certain that he will have to undergo a course of training quite foreign to his conception of sound structures as exemplified by orchestral instruments. In fact, he must start learning a new language relating to electronics, electro-acoustics and to some extent, mathematics. It is perhaps for these reasons that the whole art of electronic music appears to attract more young composers than experienced ones. For example, a composer should understand the terminology of electronics, the ease or otherwise with which he will handle this kind of equipment relating to the degree of understanding of the basic principles. This will be aided if he shows natural curiosity as to how it works. Then, he must understand audio-acoustics. Although such a study is really fundamental to most music, training is rarely given, but even with conventional instruments the use of microphones and loudspeakers is commonplace. It would be as well to have some mathematical knowledge and, if possible, to understand the arithmetic of computers and one of the common computer languages such as ALGOL or FORTRAN. However, even an understanding of the basic rules will help them to converse with computers.

It might be as well for the composer to examine the history of experimental music techniques. There are many equally valid ways of expressing the parameters of music beyond his own, and of course this leads to an examination of other media and their importance for music and art in general. Then there have been many articles, papers and books published over the past twenty years on "new" music theories and their application to the electronic medium. One may ask, where is this kind of training to be obtained? Well, in actual fact it is the electronic music studio which is the classroom and the electronic compositions produced in these studios are the text, for each and every one so far has been an experiment and no two are ever alike. It is an experimental art allied to long proven apparatus such as audio amplifiers, tape recorders and loudspeakers; they are the medium instead of orchestral players, and this leads one to consider the methods of presentation of electrically realized sound.

All such sounds can be heard only through the medium of loudspeakers. Customarily, it has been necessary to separate the performers from the listeners by some spatial relationship, usually in the form of a stage and an auditorium. In a concert hall, the sheer mass of the number of performers makes this essential. Moreover, since there is no control over the type, loudness or quality of the sound beyond that imposed by the conductor and the number of instruments, the total effect is made or marred by the physical construction of the auditorium, manifested as an acoustic phenomenon. The reverberation constant of any given building can only be modified in some rather cumbersome way by alterations of the ratio of reflected to absorbed sound, usually executed by moveable panels or reflectors. The conventional geometry tends to an audience face to face with performers.

If one considers recorded music instead of live music, then quite a casual study elicits the fact that new methods have been evolved for dealing with architectural acoustics while recording. The placing of microphones, artificial reverberation, stereo techniques, amplification procedures within specific frequency ranges and other techniques allow kinds and degrees of definition, balance and general transparency unknown in live music. Recording technique goes beyond traditional three-dimensional architectural acoustics and establishes its own frame of spatial reference, which can be manipulated by the recording engineers in a great many ways. We can of course learn from the cinema to some extent. Whereas at the introduction of sound films there were inadequate loudspeakers inadequately placed, things have advanced with multi-track recordings to the extent that, while the main loudspeakers are still behind the screen (because the interest lies there,) subsidiary units can be found in other parts of the auditorium. These may not be in use all the time, but the effect of being *immersed* in a sound field creates a quite new sensation in music and this is something which must be considered in conjunction with electronic music. Since live performances to date have been few and the exploitation techniques are uncertain, little experience has been forthcoming in the placement of loudspeakers for this specialized purpose. But it is reasonable to imagine sufficient numbers of loudspeakers to enable the composer to project his spatial ideas in the most effective manner. Intimacy is enjoyed at home with stereo record players, where one is to some extent immersed in the sound. There is no doubt in the author's mind that this is the technique for public performance. Multiple loudspeakers do not necessarily mean a very loud sound; rather they mean a total sound field, abolishing the point source effect. To take an analogy, if one enters a church when the organ is playing, the bass pedal notes seem to have no position in the building; they are all-pervading and one cannot pin-point their source. This is because of the long wavelength of the very low frequencies, tending to diffract or creep along the walls, while there may be reverberation to heighten the effect; but it is very real. And of course it is well known that the higher the frequency, the more the beam of sound tends to become a point source—certainly with conventional cone speakers. Therefore considerable thought should be given to the relationship between audience and loudspeakers in presenting electronic music. This of course tends to other techniques, the illusion of distance, for instance, by sweeping the sound from one unit to others, making it come nearer or further away from the audience. There is tremendous scope for experiment and research in this field, if only to destroy the dimensional impression inherent in the existing architectural characteristics of established concert halls. One must remember that these concert halls were built because at the time this was the only way to bring the public into contact with good music; there was no radio, no records. This phase may take its place with other milestones in history, we do not know yet; it is to some extent bound up with sociology.

In the final analysis it must be recognized that hearing is a very individual thing; no two people hear in the same way. Sometimes it is too refined, sometimes perhaps too coarse, but in any event conditioned by education and long usage. It is fortunate indeed that there is more agreement than disagreement over the character and effect of sound spectra, and this statement is made only to underline that the precision of which electronic composing systems are capable may in fact be too precise for some ears, and to suggest that the user of sophisticated apparatus should exercise patience until he is quite sure of the relationship between the calculated parameters and the effect as heard aurally.

It would appear that we require a new body of psychoacoustic data, pertaining specifically to musical problems; such studies should directly relate the properties of the acoustic wave to the perceived sound. It would supplant our limited descriptions of musical sounds which can only be given in terms of the instrument producing them. The skill required of the composer in computer music is exacting, because to work at all efficiently the composer must be able to accurately predict or "prehear" how the acoustic product will be perceived; and the ability to do this will be based largely on knowledge of the psychophysics of hearing—the relationship of intensity to loudness, of fundamental frequency to pitch, of waveform to timbre.

It will be evident to everyone that the tape recorder makes the whole art of serious electronic music possible. It may be asked why, and this is easy to answer at this time. Firstly, sound of any nature impressed on magnetic tape can be monitored, played back, reversed, edited, altered in speed (resulting in pitch changes;) other sounds or signals can be superimposed and there is little limit to the number of times that rerecording is possible. Secondly, an elementary form of machine enables a musician to experiment at home and at little cost, the only difficulty being a possible lack of synchronism between material impressed at various times. One of the most important reasons why this facility of rerecording is so necessary is that equipment currently available for musical composition or synthesis is limited as to the number of channels available. Both the cost and the difficulty of manipulation would enormously increase if complete compositions representing many parts could be constructed at once. The general practice is to compose one or two parts, then rerecord another two and so on, until the desired effect is obtained. Two has been found the optimum number of simultaneous channels for convenient operation.

It must not be overlooked that some of the sounds on a multiple tape may not be electronic in origin. One can superimpose sounds made by the voice, mouth and lips, and many other actual sounds or noises. This is one way of correcting or adding to a composition which appears to be deficient in some way. The method is made use of in live electronic music performances.

It is clear then that any serious experiments (for every new composition is virtually an experiment) must call for tape recording, and this at once leads to commercial difficulties. Why? Because the linear speed and the position of any part of the tape must be known with accuracy, and it must be possible to revert to any section of the tape within a few thousandths of an inch. This would not be possible without a synchronous driving system, and the most convenient device is tape with sprocket holes or perforations. Of course, this does not mean that standard tape is of no use, a great deal of useful exploratory work can be done with two or three ordinary tape recorders started at the same instant and impulsed with a synchronizing mark—an audible pip, or a combination of these in the form of a code.

It is worth remembering that by holding the tape one can pull it in both directions over the playback head, thus finding the exact spot required for processing, which usually means cutting the tape. This is easily accomplished with a razor blade using a special guide for the tape called a block. The length of tape one may have to play with, and some typical measurements are given in Fig. 4-15. Cuts should be made at an angle of 45° to reduce noise in the form of clicks or thumps.

Some excellent work has been done on simple apparatus of this kind. Recorders used for this purpose should have a monitoring head so that the sounds may be heard all the time from the actual tape itself. Most commercial tape recorders are driven by small ac motors of little power; unfortunately, there is no standardization in design, and we find machines with one, two or three motors. This is a defect from our point of view, since it will not be possible to obtain variable speed control. In any case, it is doubtful if the actual constancy of speed (as distinct from the irregularity of rotational speed, generally called "wow") is sufficiently accurate for sine wave processing, for it is an interesting fact that with complex waves small control movements, such as, for example, the steps between one turn of wire on a rheostat and the next, are not observed, whereas with a pure sine wave the difference in level is noticeable. Therefore the control of speed must be carried out by a more complex system, often involving servo methods where an error voltage (derived from the armature) is compared with a controlled voltage, and automatically caused to bring the speed to some assigned figure. Means are provided to alter the control voltage at will and in a stepless fashion to change the rotational speed of the tape drive system as may be required. Alternatively, the speed control may be effected by electromagnetic clutches, impulsed by automatic or manual means, and such clutches can be made very rapid in action—a few milliseconds at worst. Again, variable speed can be secured by a system of cone pulleys, which are stepless, and this is a mechanical method of considerable accuracy, especially useful over wide pitch changes, i.e., an octave or more. Clutches can operate the cones, so that, if suitable cueing or control signal are available, the recorder can stop after every note or structure has been recorded, and wait while the next tone is being set up, when another cue signal will instantly start the tape again. This is economical in tape, though it may mean a certain amount of editing later. Time, however, is one of the factors which cannot be taken into account in this art. It is naturally more economical to use a multi-track recorder if possible, for with sprocket hole tape all the channels can be ferried backwards and forwards until signals are impressed as desired, whether the method is to use many heads on one tape or separate heads on separate tapes coupled by sprockets on a common shaft. The latter arrangement makes it much easier to erase any part of one track without affecting adjacent ones. It is seen that a variable speed recorder of great accuracy is highly desirable and quite essential for some work. All the same, as already stated, some excellent work can be done on

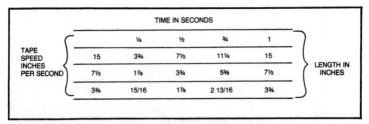

Fig. 4-15. Tape cutting measurements.

ordinary high-quality domestic recorders if suitable cueing methods are devised; of course, two tracks can be recorded at one time on a stereo machine.

In the case of computer composed music, if the studio is sufficiently complex there is no reason why a succession of chords or other complete synthesis cannot be stored and called up when required to impress on a precision recording machine using unperforated tape, provided that it has multiple heads. The main reason for specialized recorders is to ensure absolutely constant speed; not only is this desirable from a performance aspect, but if the tape holds synchronizing marks on one track or is to be fed back again into the system for re-processing, then the slightest flutter or wow might ruin an expensive composition. Where the utmost precision is called for, the frequency required for the stated motor speed can be generated by a high power electronic oscillator, when it will have a much greater accuracy than if obtained from the public service mains.

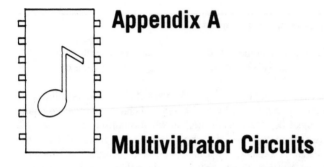

Appendix A

Multivibrator Circuits

There is a great similarity between monostable, and astable multivibrator circuits, indeed they are the same except for small changes to allow them to perform the various duties. All are pulse generators, all produce a square wave unless engineered to do otherwise. The monostable blocks itself after one cycle. The basic multivibrator circuit is a self-oscillating regenerative switch, in which the on and off periods are controlled by the C1-R1 and C2-R2 time constants. If these are equal (C1 = C2 and R1 = R2,) the circuit oscillates at a frequency of roughly. $\dfrac{1}{1.4C1R1}$ Thus, the frequency can be altered by altering either the two capacitors, or the two resistors. See Fig. A-1. The generated wave is not quite square but has rounded corners, because the collector voltage of each transistor cannot rise immediately to the supply rail as it turns off, since it is loaded by the cross-coupling capacitor. To get this circuit to oscillate, the two halves must be slightly out of balance, so that one transistor starts before the other when the line voltage is applied. If they both started simultaneously, no oscillations would be produced.

Since the monostable is used to initiate percussion and other musical circuits, it is explained here. Q1 is normally cut off, Q2 is driven to saturation via R1, and C1 is fully charged. When the switch contact S1 is closed (momentarily,) Q1 is now driven to saturation and Q2 is turned off by the resulting negative-going charge of C1. As soon as this action is complete, C1 starts to discharge through R1 until its charge falls to such a low value that Q2 starts to turn on again; this second regenerative action causes the transistors to revert to their original state. The length of the pulse so generated is fixed by the values of R1 and C1 and is roughly $0.7 \times C1 \times R1$ if C is in μF and R is in kilohms; the time of the pulse (p) will be in

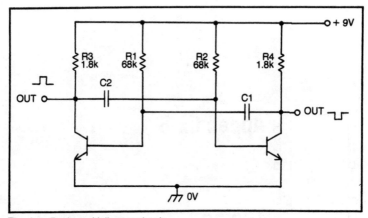

Fig. A-1. Basic multivibrator circuit.

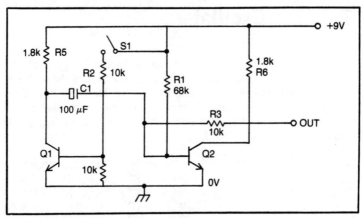

Fig. A-2. Multivibrator with Manual Start.

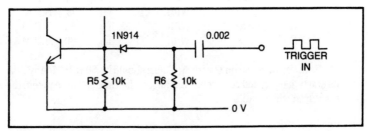

Fig. A-3. Electronic start for a multivibrator.

microseconds. If the initiating switch is held on, or pressed again before the cycle is complete, it will not give out a single pulse but may run on in a random fashion. The circuit is as easily triggered by any wave which is not sinusoidal (see Figs. A-2 and A-3.)

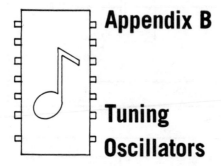

Appendix B

Tuning
Oscillators

To tune independent oscillators (C 261.6 to 523.2 octave.) The procedure is to tune each pair to zero beat. Then flatten by the amount shown. Never tune flat and then sharpen. Use a flute sound, never reeds or strings. Start with A (440 Hz) exact to tuning fork or stable oscillator. Then take E (below) and hold with A to 89 beats per minute. Next take B above, hold with the E just tuned to 67 B.P.M.

Then	F$^{\#}$	Below	With	B	To	100	B.P.M.
Then	C$^{\#}$	Below	With	F$^{\#}$	To	75	B.P.M.
Then	G$^{\#}$	Above	With	C$^{\#}$	To	56	B.P.M.
Then	D$^{\#}$	Below	With	G$^{\#}$	To	84	B.P.M.
Then	A$^{\#}$	Above	With	D$^{\#}$	To	63	B.P.M.
Then	F	Below	With	A$^{\#}$	To	94	B.P.M.
Then	C	Below	With	F	To	71	B.P.M.
Then	G	Above	With	C	To	53	B.P.M.
Then	D	Below	With	G	To	80	B.P.M.

A check can be made on D with A. There should be 60 B.P.M. Any drift means starting over, and remember the longer the time and care taken, the more accurate the results.

Appendix C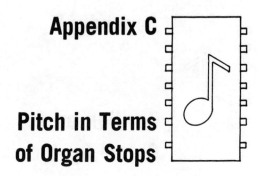

Pitch in Terms of Organ Stops

NOTE	C	C¹	G¹	C²
FREQUENCY. Hz	130.8	261.6	392	523.3
RATIO TO FUNDAMENTAL	1:2	1	3:2	2:1
HARMONIC NUMBER		1		2
DESIGNATION AS ORGAN STOP	16 FT	8	5 1/3	4
NAME OR DESCRIPTION	SUB FUNDAMENTAL	FUNDAMENTAL	QUINT	OCTAVE

NOTE	G²	C³	E³	G³	A³
FREQUENCY Hz	784	1046	1319	1568	1865
RATIO TO FUNDAMENTAL	3:1	4:1	5:1	6:1	7:1
HARMONIC NUMBER	3	4	5	6	7
DESIGNATION AS ORGAN STOP	2 2/3	2	1 3/5	1 1/3	1 1/7
NAME OR DESCRIPTION	TWELFTH	FIFTEENTH	TIERCE	LARIGOT	SEPTIEME

Fig. C. Pitch in terms of organ stops; based on middle C A = 440 Hz.

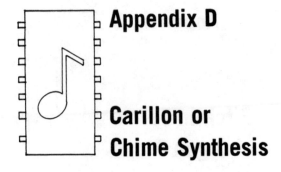

Appendix D

Carillon or Chime Synthesis

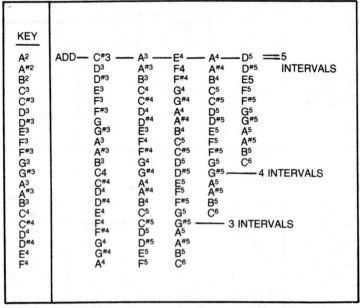

KEY	ADD					
A^2	$C^{\#}3$	A^3	E^4	A^4	D^5	═5 INTERVALS
$A^{\#}2$	D^3	$A^{\#}3$	$F4$	$A^{\#}4$	$D^{\#}5$	INTERVALS
B^2	$D^{\#}3$	B^3	$F^{\#}4$	B^4	$E5$	
C^3	E^3	C^4	G^4	C^5	$F5$	
$C^{\#}3$	F^3	$C^{\#}4$	$G^{\#}4$	$C^{\#}5$	$F^{\#}5$	
D^3	$F^{\#}3$	D^4	A^4	D^5	G^5	
$D^{\#}3$	G	$D^{\#}4$	$A^{\#}4$	$D^{\#}5$	$G^{\#}5$	
E^3	$G^{\#}3$	E^3	B^4	E^5	A^5	
F^3	A^3	F^4	C^5	F^5	$A^{\#}5$	
$F^{\#}3$	$A^{\#}3$	$F^{\#}4$	$C^{\#}5$	$F^{\#}5$	B^5	
G^3	B^3	G^4	D^5	G^5	C^6	
$G^{\#}3$	$C4$	$G^{\#}4$	$D^{\#}5$	$G^{\#}5$	——— 4 INTERVALS	
A^3	$C^{\#}4$	A^4	E^5	A^5		
$A^{\#}3$	D^4	$A^{\#}4$	$F5$	$A^{\#}5$		
B^3	$D^{\#}4$	B^4	$F^{\#}5$	B^5		
C^4	E^4	C^5	G^5	C^6		
$C^{\#}4$	F^4	$C^{\#}5$	$G^{\#}5$ ——— 3 INTERVALS			
D^4	$F^{\#}4$	D^5	A^5			
$D^{\#}4$	G^4	$D^{\#}5$	$A^{\#}5$			
E^4	$G^{\#}4$	E^5	B^5			
F^4	A^4	$F5$	C^6			

Fig. D. Carillon or chime synthesis (note: sine waves required.)

Bibliography

Anfilov, G. *Physics & Music*. Mir Publishers, Moscow.

Babbit, Milton. "The Synthesis, Perception and Specification of Musical Time," *International Folk Music*, Vol. 16, 1964.

Babbit, Milton. *"The Use of Computers in Musicological Research"*. Princeton University Press, Princeton, N.J., 1965.

Badings, H. and J.W. de Bruyn. *Philips Technical Review*, Vol. 19, No. 6, 1957.

Bateman, Wayne. *Introduction to Computer Music*. J. Wiley & Sons.

Beauchamp, J.W. *Generation of New Electronic Sounds*. Technical report No. 7, University of Illinois.

Blackey, C. "IC's for Electro-Music," *Electronics & Music Maker*. April, 1981.

Brun, Herbert. "Technology and the Composer." *UNESCO Conference on Music and Technology*, Stockholm, June, 1970.

Button, C. "Syntom Drum Synthesizer," *E & MM*. April, 1981.

Cakulev & Borislav. "High Performance Voltage to Frequency Converter," *Electronic Engineering*. March, 1969.

Casserley, L. "Electronic Music Techniques," *E & MM*. June, 1981.

Chamberlin, H. *Musical Applications of Microprocessors*. Hayden Book Co.

Ciamaga, Gustav. "Training of the Composer in New Technological Means," *UNESCO Conference on Music and Technology*. Stockholm, June, 1970. Gustav Ciamaga and J. Gabura, University of Toronto, Canada.

Conly, P. and Razdow, A. *Digital Composition and Control of an Electronic Music Synthesizer*. 41st AES Convention 1971.

Douglas, A. *Electrical Production of Music*. Philosophical Library, New York, 1957.

Douglas, A. "Electronic Synthesis of Musical Tones," *Electronic Engineering*. July to Sept., 1953.

Douglas, A. "Synthetic Music," *Electronic Engineering*. 1956.

Douglas, A. "Percussion Circuits for Electronic Musical Instruments," *Electronic Engineering*. 30, July, 1958.

Enkel, F. *Tech Hausmitt NWDR*, Vol. 6, Nos. 42-46, 1954.

Forte, A. "A Programme for Analytic Reading of Scores," *J. Music Theory*, No. 10, 1966.

Gurvitch, G. "Les Variations des Perceptions Collectives des Entendues," *Cahiers Internationaux de Soliologie*, Vol. 37, 1964.

Hill, V.S. "Guide to Electronic Music Techniques," *E & MM*. April, 1981.

Hiller, L.A. and Baker, R.A. "Automated Music Printing," *J. Music Theory*. No. 9, 1865.

Hiller, L.A. and Isaacson, L.M. *Experimental Music*. McGraw-Hill Book Co. New York.

Jacobi, H. and Schmidt, A. "Reaktanzvierpole als Filter," *V.N.*, Vol. 2, 1932. *Journal Audio Eng. Soc.* New York.

Jordan, C. "Advanced Music Synthesis," *E & MM*. April, 1981.

Kaegi, Werner. "Music and Technology in the Europe of 1970." *UNESCO Conference on Music and Technology*. Stockholm, June, 1970.

Knight, G. "Micro-Music," *E & MM*. May, 1981.

Koenig, G. M. "The Use of Computer Programmes in Creating Music," *UNESCO Conference on Music and Technology*. Stockholm, June, 1970.

Lewis and MacLaren, *J. Soc. Motion Picture Eng*, Vol. 50, No. 3.

MacCaulay, J. "Hi-Fi Bass Woofer," *E & MM*. March, 1981.

Matthews, Max. "Electronic Sound Studio of the 1970's," *UNESCO Conference on Music and Technology*. Stockholm, June, 1970.

Matthews, Max. *Music by Computers*. Cambridge, Mass.

Matthews, Pierce, and Gutman. *Gravsaner Blatter*, No. 23, 1962.

Meyer-Eppler, W. *Elektronische Musik*. Berlin, 1955.

Meyer-Eppler, W. "Elektronisches Kompositions Technik," *Melos*, Vol. 20, 1953.

Moles, Abraham. "Informationstheorie der Musik," *Nachtenrichtentechnische Fachberichte*, Vol. 3. Braunschweig, 1946.

Moog, Robert A. "A Voltage Controlled Lowpass Highpass Filter for Audio Signal Processing," *J. Audio Eng Soc*. 1965.

Moog, Robert A. "Voltage Controlled Electronic Modules," *J. Audio Eng Soc*, Vol. 13, No. 3, 1965.

Music, Physics and Engineering. Dover Publishing Inc., New York.

Olson, H. F. and Belar, H. *J. Acoustical Soc America*. Vol. 33, No. 9.

Pinkerton, R. C. *Scientific American*, Vol. 194, No. 2, 1956.

Risset, J. C. *An Introductory Catalogue of Computer Sounds*. Bell Telephone Laboratories, Murray Hill, N.J.

Sala, O. "Experimentalle Grundlagen des Trautoniums," *Frequenz*, Vol. 2, 1932.

Schaeffer, Pierre. "La Musique et les Ordinateurs," *UNESCO Conference on Music and Technology*. Stockholm, June, 1970.

Seashore, C. A. *Psychology of Music*. Dover Publishing, New York; Constable, London, 1968.

Shannon and Weaver. *Mathematical Theory of Communication*. University of Illinois Press, Urbana, 1949.

Shibata, Minao. "Music and Technology in Japan," *UNESCO Conference on Music and Technology*. Stockholm, June, 1970.

Trautwein, F. *Elektronische Musik*. Verlag Weidmann, Berlin, 1930.

Trautwein, F. "Toneinsatz und electronische Musik," *Z. Tech Phys*, No. 13, 1932.

Ussachevsky, V. A. *J. Audio Eng Soc New York*, Vol. 6, No. 3.

Winckel, F. "Electronische Steurung multivariabler Räume," *Buhnentechnische Rundschau*, No. 2, 1967.

Xenaxia, I. "Musique Formelles," *La Revue Musicale*. 253, Paris, 1968.

Zinovieff, P. *A Computerized Music Studio*. Electronic Music Report, Inst of Sonology, Utrecht State University, 1969.

Zinovieff, P. "The Special Case of Inspirational Computer Music Scores," *London Magazine*. July, 1969.

Index

Edited by Roland Phelps